HOURS OF OPPORTUNITY

VOLUME 2

The Power of Data to Improve After-School Programs Citywide

JENNIFER SLOAN **MCCOMBS** NATE **ORR** SUSAN J. **BODILLY** SCOTT **NAFTEL**
LOUAY **CONSTANT** ETHAN **SCHERER** DANIEL **GERSHWIN**

T0150145

Commissioned by

The Wallace Foundation

Supporting ideas.
Sharing solutions.
Expanding opportunities.

RAND EDUCATION

The research in this report was produced within RAND Education, a unit of the RAND Corporation. The research was commissioned by The Wallace Foundation.

Library of Congress Cataloging-in-Publication Data

Hours of opportunity / Susan J. Bodilly.
  v. cm.
  Includes bibliographical references and index.
  Contents: v. 1. Lessons from five cities on building systems to improve after-school, summer school, and other out-of-school-time programs
  ISBN 978-0-8330-5048-9 (v. 1) -- ISBN 978-0-8330-5049-6 (v. 2)
    1. After-school programs—United States—Case studies. 2. Summer school—United States—Case studies. 3. School improvement programs—United States—Case studies. I. Bodilly, Susan J.

  LC34.4.H68 2010
  371.8—dc22

                      2010031804

Cover design by Pete Soriano

Published 2010 by the RAND Corporation
1776 Main Street, P.O. Box 2138, Santa Monica, CA 90407-2138
1200 South Hayes Street, Arlington, VA 22202-5050
4570 Fifth Avenue, Suite 600, Pittsburgh, PA 15213-2665
RAND URL: http://www.rand.org/
To order RAND documents or to obtain additional information, contact
Distribution Services: Telephone: (310) 451-7002;
Fax: (310) 451-6915; Email: order@rand.org

Preface

High-quality out-of-school-time (OST) programs, which for the purposes here include after-school and summer programs, have the potential to help children and youth develop to their fullest potential. However, the OST systems that provide such programs in U.S. cities still suffer from fragmentation and lack of coordination. The result is often poor access and poor quality for those most in need of these services. A key contributor to these systems' ongoing fragmentation is a lack of shared information regarding youth participation, attendance, and OST programming.

In an effort to spur the creation of citywide systems of high-quality OST programs, The Wallace Foundation established an out-of-school learning initiative to fund OST system-building efforts in five cities—Boston, Chicago, New York City, Providence, and Washington, D.C. A key requirement of the initiative was for the cities to build an information, technology, and communication infrastructure to facilitate management and support of OST programs. In January 2008, The Wallace Foundation asked the RAND Corporation to document the progress of these cities toward their goals and to examine the development and use of management information (MI) systems to track participation.

This monograph reviews the adoption of MI systems in the OST field by examining the use of these systems by OST providers and city-level policymakers in eight case-study cities. In addition to the five Wallace initiative cities, the assessment includes Denver, Louisville, and San Francisco. It examines why MI systems were adopted, the current status of implementation, how data from the MI systems are used by various stakeholders, and factors that enable or hinder use of those data. Two companion publications, *Hours of Opportunity*, Volume 1: *Lessons from Five Cities on Building Systems to Improve After-School, Summer School, and Other Out-of-School-Time Programs* (Bodilly et al., 2010) and *Hours of Opportunity*, Volume 3: *Profiles of Five Cities Improving After-School Programs Through a Systems Approach* (McCombs et al., 2010), focus on the system-building efforts of the five Wallace-funded cities and present detailed case studies, respectively. The findings of the study should be of interest to policymakers and practitioners involved in improving OST services, especially at the local city level.

This research was conducted by RAND Education, a unit of the RAND Corporation.

The research sponsor, The Wallace Foundation, seeks to support and share effective ideas and practices to improve learning and enrichment opportunities for children. Its current objectives are to improve the quality of schools, primarily by developing and placing effective principals in high-need schools; improve the quality of and access to out-of-school-time programs through coordinated city systems and by strengthening the financial management skills of providers; integrate in- and out-of-school learning by supporting efforts to reimagine and expand learning time during the traditional school day and year as well as during the summer months, helping expand access to arts learning, and using technology as a tool for teaching and promoting creativity and imagination. For more information and research on these and related topics, please visit The Wallace Foundation Knowledge Center at www.wallacefoundation.org.

Contents

Tables

Summary

All cities strive to ensure that children and youth develop into healthy, productive members of society. Out-of-school-time (OST) programs, which for our purposes include after-school and summer learning programs, have been increasingly seen as helping cities and states meet this goal. Research has shown that high-quality OST programs are associated with improvements in children's attendance, homework completion, grades, school behavior, and socioemotional outcomes (Lauer et al., 2006). In addition, OST programs may reduce crime and teen pregnancy rates by engaging youth after school hours, prime time for teens, in particular, to engage in problem behaviors (Fight Crime: Invest in Kids, 2000; U.S. Department of Education and U.S. Department of Justice, 2000).

Within cities, OST programming can be fragmented and uncoordinated. OST providers rely on an unsteady and often insufficient patchwork of city, state, federal, and private funding and user fees. Further, in many cities that provide financial support for OST, funding is funneled through a variety of youth-serving agencies that lack basic information about the programs they fund, such as the number of students served and program attendance. The result can be suboptimal provision: Those most in need of these services often have limited access to programs, and available programming is often not of the highest quality. Increasingly, researchers and supporters of these programs have advocated for more systemic efforts around OST provision as a method to improve quality and access (Halpern, 2006). One function of an OST "system" can be to create mechanisms that enable the flow of information among key stakeholders to improve decision-making. Management information (MI) systems are one such mechanism, enabling the collecting and sharing of data.

The MI systems described in this monograph are web-based and used, at a minimum, to collect and organize data on OST program activities, participant demographics, and participant enrollment and attendance. Providers enter data on an ongoing basis, and the systems typically include a series of built-in reports, allowing city-level funders (often city youth-serving agencies or intermediaries) and providers to track program performance throughout a program session and at the end of a session. These systems may or may not be linked to other data systems, such as a school district data system.

In the absence of these web-based MI systems, providers either record enrollment, attendance, and program data on paper or use a static computing system that can be operated from only one computer at the provider site. Under these conditions, city managers often do not receive data from providers until after a session has ended.

Data from MI systems can lead to improved access and services, which could, in turn, lead to better participant outcomes in two ways. At the city level, current information on enrollment and participation gives city managers rough indicators of both a program's interest to students (enrollment) and its quality (participation). City managers can use this information to identify potentially struggling programs and intercede with support, determine which programs or types of programs to fund based on historical enrollment figures, and place programs in specific areas of the city with higher demand. Second, providers can use their own data to modify programs midcourse, follow up with students to encourage participation, and plan future programs more effectively.

Purpose of This Study

In an effort to spur the creation of citywide systems of high-quality OST programs, The Wallace Foundation established an out-of-school learning initiative to fund OST system-building efforts in five major

U.S. cities—Boston, Chicago, New York City, Providence, and Washington, D.C. A requirement of this effort was that the cities adopt MI systems to support OST programs and system building. The Foundation asked the RAND Corporation to study the cities' progress toward their goals and to provide an assessment of the use of MI systems in these and other cities.

This monograph addresses the second part of the RAND study and examines the use of MI systems by OST providers and city-level policymakers in eight case-study cities. Five of the cities were Wallace initiative sites; the three others were Denver, Louisville, and San Francisco. Findings from the first part of the study are reported in *Hours of Opportunity*, Volume 1: *Lessons from Five Cities on Building Systems to Improve After-School, Summer School, and Other Out-of-School-Time Programs* (Bodily et al., 2010), which examines the system-building efforts in the Wallace initiative sites. A third RAND publication, *Hours of Opportunity*, Volume 3: *Profiles of Five Cities Improving After-School Programs Through a Systems Approach* (McCombs et al., 2010), presents case studies of the Wallace-funded cities' efforts under the grant, including the development and implementation of MI systems.

This monograph presents insights from eight cities and is structured around three overarching research questions:

1. Why and how were MI systems for OST adopted in citywide efforts?
2. How are cities' MI systems currently used and implemented by various OST stakeholders?
   - What is the current status of implementation in these cities?
   - What do cities do to ensure data quality?
   - How and to what extent do city-level officials and providers use data from MI systems?
3. What factors have enabled or hindered implementation?

Data and Methods

We use descriptive case analyses of eight major U.S. cities to investigate issues surrounding MI system adoption and use by city agencies, intermediaries, and OST providers. Because this monograph was produced as part of a larger study investigating system-building efforts in cities funded through The Wallace Foundation initiative, it includes the five Wallace-funded cities. However, The Foundation was interested in how other cities had adopted MI systems independent of the initiative. These cities were not selected to serve as contrasts or comparisons for the Wallace-funded cities, nor did we ensure that the sample was representative of all cities that have adopted MI systems to track OST programs. We identified potential additional cities through a literature review and interviews with officials from the National League of Cities and major vendors of MI systems used in OST programs. We also conducted a brief interview with a leader in each of the eight cities to determine the scale, scope, and use of each MI system and the leader's willingness to participate in the study. In consultation with Wallace Foundation staff, we selected the additional cities based on a number of factors, including where the city was geographically located and how it used its MI system. In addition, we attempted to avoid cities that were already participating in another Wallace-funded study regarding the participation of middle school youth in OST programs. Collectively, the eight cities provide illustrative examples of the development and implementation of MI systems to improve OST provision.

For each of the case studies, we interviewed a range of city leaders, including representatives from city agencies that funded OST programs, the mayor's office, the school district central office, and intermediary organizations, as well as OST providers, after-school coordinators, and principals. Across the eight sites, we conducted 168 interviews. In addition, we administered a survey to providers in each city except Boston, where the survey was not applicable because the MI system was still in development. We analyzed interview data around themes derived from prior literature and conducted descriptive statistical analyses of the survey data.

Findings

The OST field is relatively new to developing MI systems and using the data to inform decisionmaking. At the time of our last round of data collection, in spring 2009, the case-study cities did not consider their work in this area to be complete, but all had made substantial progress. We found that city officials and OST providers shared a vision of how MI systems could gather information to support system improvement. The specific findings are summarized here.

City context drove development decisions. Each city had a unique context and goals that shaped some overarching development decisions. Cities' initial goals (e.g., to improve contract management, to coordinate in-school and after-school program data) led varying proportions of OST providers to use the MI system and to the presence or absence of data linkages with other information systems in the city. Varying desire for control over the data led to differing decisions regarding whether to develop the MI system in-house or to contract with an external vendor.

MI systems evolved over time. Many of the cities made modifications to enhance their MI systems over time. Cities developed new types of capabilities in their systems, such as the ability to process requests for proposals; changed the type of data gathered; and worked to make the system more user-friendly. Changes in context in two cities (Boston and Washington, D.C.) led to the adoption of new MI systems to meet new or growing needs.

MI systems gave cities much-needed data about OST programming and participation, which they used to improve programs. All the cities used data from their MI systems to better understand OST programming and participation (e.g., enrollment, attendance, demographics). The importance of this use cannot be underestimated. Prior to MI system adoption, the cities could say little about the programs they funded or the youth being served. As one interviewee noted,

> The biggest benefit is knowing what we are buying with these programs because, for so many years, we worked off our projections and aggregate numbers provided by CBOs. When we went to real data, our numbers dropped to like 40,000 kids. The ben-

efit has been that now we know who we are reaching, how often, and how much money we are spending.

City officials put this information to work to improve participation and programming. For instance, funding partners in Denver used MI system data to identify population groups prone to dropping out of OST programs and found that middle school students were particularly likely to drop out of programming. Subsequently, the partners worked with OST site coordinators to design programs that would better engage this age group.

MI system data improved OST contract management and shifted its nature to focus on the quality of programming. Agency and intermediary leaders in Chicago, New York City, San Francisco, and Washington, D.C., all reported using MI system data to improve contract management. For instance, the funding agency in San Francisco (Department of Children, Youth, and Their Families) used MI system data to manage contracts with grant recipients and to remit payments through a monthly invoicing feature.

In New York City and Chicago, we were told that the collection and use of data had shifted the nature of contract management. According to interviewees, prior to implementing their MI systems, the cities' management of OST providers was strictly contractual and focused on "paper" rather than programs. With MI system data, they were able to focus on program quality as well. For instance, city managers used average daily attendance reports to identify potential quality problems. If attendance rates dropped below certain levels, managers followed up with providers to determine whether there were problems that needed to be addressed.

Cities used MI system data to make funding decisions and to lobby for additional funding. Two cities used MI system data to inform how they funded providers. In Providence, intermediary leaders used past enrollment reports as one source of information during funding review meetings. New York City formally used its MI system as a basis for provider compensation and reduced funding to providers that did not meet attendance targets.

Agencies and intermediaries also reported using MI system data to justify their petitions for continued or additional funding. In Providence, the intermediary presented MI system reports to its board of directors, the city council, and funders, and it also used the reports to raise support for city OST efforts. In Denver, the public schools and other funding partners used results from the annual evaluations conducted by an independent evaluator, which showed a positive relationship between OST participation and school outcomes, to highlight the importance of increasing investment in the city's youth services. In New York City, the main funding agency reported using MI system information on programming and students served to help generate increased funding from the city. In fact, the agency's OST budget grew from $46.6 million in fiscal year (FY) 2006 to $118.2 million in FY 2009. As one respondent noted,

> Our agency competes for dollars against other social service agencies. Because our agency has data that demonstrate the programs that are funded and the students that are served, our agency holds a competitive advantage above others.

Sharing data from the MI systems led to greater coordination among stakeholders. We found a wide range of OST data-sharing agreements across the study sites. Some cities shared MI system reports with other city agencies but did not link the MI system to other data systems. For instance, in New York City, the main funding agency shared OST participation information with another agency serving younger children (birth to school age). This data sharing allowed the two agencies to track and understand the continuation of services for eligible children from early childhood through their school years. Data were also shared with the city's department of education.

Other cities established agreements to link the MI system data to school outcomes to enable studies of the relationship between OST participation and children and youth outcomes. Providence, Louisville, and Denver each linked MI system data to school district data and studied the links between OST participation and school outcomes. Similarly, several agencies in Washington, D.C., including the intermediary, agreed to participate in data sharing through the city's Office of the Chief Technology Officer to link school district, OST participation, and health and human services data.

Mayoral demand for data appeared to be a key enabler of the cities' use of data. Resources, particularly time, were limited for city officials. Without a demand for data at the highest levels, some found it difficult to prioritize analyzing data even when they desired to do so. However, mayoral demand for data required city officials to set aside time and prioritize activities and resources in order to analyze, report, and use the MI system data. For instance, in New York City, agencies ensured that data were entered into the MI system and developed the capacity to analyze those data to provide regular progress reports to the mayor's office.

All cities invested in efforts to improve data quality. Data quality is important if an MI system is to be an effective tool to improve OST programming. Cities took a variety of approaches to ensuring the quality of entered data. Two cities uploaded participant data from district databases to ensure the accuracy of student records. Some city officials touted having participants scan their own identification cards as a highly reliable method of collecting attendance data. With these systems, attendance data were automatically entered into the MI system, preventing many data-entry errors. However, we found the scan technology to be underused by providers in the cities that supported it.

All cities invested in training users, including OST providers and city staff, on how to use the MI system. New York City and San Francisco also created intermediate and advanced training sessions for OST executive directors and program managers (individuals in charge of a program or group of programs) that covered data analysis, interpretation, and the creation of summary reports. Providers reported substantial demand for MI system training and were particularly interested in more advanced training in how to analyze, interpret, and share information.

Many providers reported using data from MI systems; however, they also reported constraints that limited their use of the data. The majority of providers agreed that their city's MI system provided valuable information about OST programs and reported a number of uses for the data, including program management, program improvement, providing information to funders, and lobbying for additional funding. As one San Francisco provider explained,

> Although data entry can put a strain on the agency due to time restrictions (not enough time for staff to enter data), the programs greatly benefit from the information derived from the [MI system]. The information helps in many ways, such as program management, program evaluation, program planning and fund development, and quality assurance.

However, even when there was support for the MI system, a few providers described capacity constraints that limited their use of data. According to one provider,

> In my opinion, the whole concept of management information systems is fundamentally sound and will eventually become extremely useful. However, for small organizations like ours, unless funding and personnel problems are solved, it will be challenging to get the most out of the system. For now, it is a tool we see as being very useful up the road. We see potential and hope to be able to take advantage of it in the near future.

Providers who did not feel that the city MI system was useful tended to perceive it as oriented toward contract management and compliance. One provider expressed this sentiment plainly: "This system was not designed to help me. It is used by someone else to monitor me. Therefore, its usefulness to me is lost."

Some providers reported having to use one or more additional MI systems for other funders or to support their own organization's improvement needs, which was negatively related to providers' views of the city MI system. Survey respondents explained the difficulties and frustration of using multiple MI systems. As one provider explained,

> We all understand the need for management information systems. However, when an organization is funded by federal, state, and city contracts and each . . . requires a management information system, our staff have to enter the same client information

. . . into five different databases. Government agencies need to collaborate better and have a coordinated management information effort. It is a waste of staff time to enter the same information into so many databases—and this is an activity that no government grant is willing to pay for.

Finally, providers who had been using the city MI system longer were more likely to view it positively. This suggests that there is a learning curve associated with a new MI system and that perceptions of usefulness improve after the first year.

Lessons for an Emerging Field

While each of the sites experienced the development and implementation of MI systems in different ways, many of the factors that constrained or enabled the systems' use were shared. These experiences point to the following lessons for other cities interested in improving OST provision through the use of data:

- *MI systems are capable of supporting OST system improvement but will not do so without careful planning.* Cities in the study faced a number of decisions during the development phase that affected the ways in which the MI systems could be used. The lesson is that a clear understanding of the goals for the data, including how those goals support larger OST system-building goals, is a prerequisite for an effective MI system. In addition, it might be necessary to modify the MI system based on experience to enhance its utility. Likewise, cities had to adopt methods of breaking down barriers to the systems' use, such as training, dedication of staff time for data analysis, or the hiring of external evaluators.
- *Using data to showcase OST efforts can lead to additional funding and support.* City leaders and providers reported that the ability to show their funders enrollment, participation, and outcome data led to increases in resources and provided them with a competitive advantage over others seeking funding.

- *Customization of web-based systems encouraged MI system use.* MI system users typically thought the systems were easy to use and said that the web-based interface, implemented in all the cities we examined, encouraged timely data entry because the system could be accessed from multiple locations. Moreover, customization of the MI systems to meet the specific needs of city agencies and providers led to greater use of the systems and their data.
- *Investing in high-quality training reaps benefits.* Providers who reported receiving high-quality training were more likely than others to believe that the city MI system was useful. All cities offered training to providers and to city-level program officers to familiarize them with the MI system. Providers' demand for training was high, and they particularly wanted more advanced training in data analysis and the use of data.
- *Mechanisms to eliminate redundancies in data entry and reporting requirements would help providers.* One of the most significant constraints to providers' use of MI system data was the burden of entering the same data into multiple MI systems, which could include the city's MI system, another city's MI system, their organization's MI system, and a private funder's MI system. One solution would be for cities to engage in better coordination across major city organizations and to implement a common MI system. Another option would be to configure the city's MI system to allow providers to enter additional data required by other funders or their own organizations. A third option is to allow providers to easily exchange data between the city's OST MI system and other MI systems that providers might use.

Acknowledgments

Many individuals contributed to this study, which was made possible by the interest and support of the sponsor, The Wallace Foundation. In particular, we thank Zakia Redd, Ann Stone, and Ed Pauly from The Foundation's evaluation team; Nancy Devine, Sheila Murphy, and Dara Rose from the communities team; and Pam Mendenal and Lucas Held from the communication team. All provided important feedback that improved the content of this monograph.

We are particularly grateful for the cooperation and support provided by each of the cities in the study—Boston, Chicago, Denver, Louisville, New York, Providence, San Francisco, and Washington, D.C. Our respondents' willingness to share their successes and challenges in this area will aide other cities in their efforts to improve OST program provision. Reviews by city agency and intermediary staff also improved the accuracy and presentation of this monograph. We are indebted to all the individuals who participated in the study and shared their valuable time and insights with us. We particularly thank all the providers who answered the survey with such thoughtfulness.

In addition, we extend our thanks to the representatives from OST MI system vendors Cayen, Cityspan, EZ Reports, and KidTrax who spoke with us about their products and the field in general.

We appreciate the insightful reviews and comments provided by Elizabeth Reisner and RAND colleagues John Pane and Julie Marsh. The clarity of this monograph benefited greatly from their comments and suggestions.

This report would not have been completed without the assistance of many other RAND colleagues, including Vicki Park, Bing Han, Melissa Bradley, Dahlia Lichter, and Kate Giglio.

Abbreviations

CBO	community-based organization
CPS	Chicago Public Schools
DCYF	San Francisco Department of Children, Youth, and Their Families
DELTAS	Boston Public Schools Department of Extended Learning Time, Afterschool, and Services
DYCD	New York City Department of Youth and Community Development
FSS	Chicago Family and Support Services
FY	fiscal year
IT	information technology
LOAS	Lights on After School
MI	management information
OST	out-of-school time
PASA	Providence After School Alliance
RFP	request for proposals

CHAPTER ONE

Introduction

All cities strive to ensure that children and youth develop into healthy, productive members of society. Out-of-school-time (OST) programs, which include after-school and summer programs, are increasingly seen as a contributor to helping cities and states meet this goal. Research has shown that high-quality OST programs are associated with improvements in children's attendance, homework completion, grades, school behavior, and socioemotional outcomes (Lauer et al., 2006). In addition, OST programs may reduce crime and teen pregnancy by engaging youth after school hours, prime time for teens, in particular, to engage in problem behaviors (Fight Crime: Invest in Kids, 2000; U.S. Department of Education and U.S. Department of Justice, 2000).

Current State of OST Provision and Adoption of System-Building Approaches

Across the United States, an estimated 6.5 million children participate in OST programs (Afterschool Alliance, undated). OST programs offer a range of experiences for young people, focusing on academic support, arts, music, sports, technology, leadership, and socioemotional development. They can take place before school, after school, over the weekends, or during the summer. Some programs are "comprehensive," offering a variety of academic and enrichment opportunities, while others are highly specialized (e.g., robotics programs). Community-based organizations (CBOs) offer the majority of OST programming, although some city agencies, such as parks and recreation departments and libraries, also run OST programs.

Within cities, OST provision can be fragmented and uncoordinated (Halpern, 2002; Proscio and Whiting, 2004). Providers rely on an unsteady and often insufficient patchwork of city, state, federal, and private funding and user fees. Further, in many cities, public funding is funneled through a variety of youth-serving agencies without interagency coordination. Even within city agencies responsible for contracting with direct providers, a deficiency of data can lead to an inability to accurately report very basic information about the efficacy of their funding choices: how many students are served, the characteristics of those students, and their attendance rates and patterns. The result is a limited understanding of the level of supply and demand within a city, limited access to programs for those most in need of services, and programming that may not be of the highest quality (Halpern, 2006).

Increasingly, researchers and OST supporters have advocated for more systemic coordination efforts around OST to improve quality and access (Halpern, 2006, 2002; Tolman et al., 2002; Pittman, Wilson-Ahlstrom, and Yohalem, 2003). These efforts, also called system building, can be characterized by "increased interrelationships and interdependence among providers, clients, funders, and the larger community to ensure a more coherent and more regular pattern of service to meet needs" (Bodilly and Beckett, 2005, p. xxx).

One function of an OST "system" is to create mechanisms that enable the flow of information among key stakeholders to improve decisionmaking. Each city shares a broad goal for OST: to engage children and youth in high-quality, high-interest opportunities that promote their well-being and development beyond school hours. However, in the OST field, outcomes are driven by interorganizational relationships and are "produced not by a process of decision making within a single firm but by complicated networks of interacting organizations and parts of organizations" (Cyert and March, 1992, p. 233). For OST provision to be optimal, all stakeholders involved in OST must make effective decisions, both for themselves and as a group. For example, cities' legislators, agencies, and intermediaries need to make decisions about which providers and services to fund; providers need to make decisions about program content; schools need to determine which programs to offer, if any; and parents and youth need to decide whether to enroll in OST programming and in which programs to enroll. Each needs information about the others to be most effective in making these decisions.

Since the late 1990s, web-based management information (MI) systems have been developed and used to track OST participation. Prior to web-based systems (or in absence of their adoption), records were kept on paper or on a fixed computing resource (i.e., one computer that had the required software). A growing number of city agencies, intermediaries, and school districts require providers to enter data into MI systems in order to better manage OST and other programs. In addition, some provider organizations have adopted MI systems for their own internal purposes to track their services and outcomes. This trend reflects a larger movement in the private and public sectors to use information technology to manage data, produce reports, and analyze data to promote data-based decisionmaking.

When providers enter data into web-based MI systems on an ongoing basis, it allows those with access to the data (typically, providers and the funding city agency) to track data throughout an OST program session as opposed to just reviewing data at the end of a session. MI systems usually include a series of built-in reports, allowing providers and city agencies to easily track program performance. They may or may not be linked to other data systems, such as a school district data system.

Using data from MI systems in decisionmaking can lead to improved access and services, which could, in turn, lead to better participant outcomes in two ways. At the city level, current information on enrollment and participation gives city managers a rough measure of a program's interest to students (enrollment) and quality (participation). City managers can use this information to identify potentially struggling programs and intercede with support, determine which programs or types of programs to fund based on historical enrollment figures, and place programs in specific areas of the city with higher demand. Second, providers can use their own data to modify programs midcourse, follow up with students to encourage participation, and plan future programs more effectively.

Goals and Value of This Study

In an effort to spur the creation of citywide systems of high-quality OST programs, The Wallace Foundation established an out-of-school learning initiative to fund OST system-building efforts in five major U.S. cities—Boston, Chicago, New York City, Providence, and Washington, D.C. A requirement of this system-building effort was that cities adopt an MI system to facilitate better management and support for OST programs. The Wallace Foundation asked the RAND Corporation to study the progress that funded cities had made toward their goals and to provide an assessment of the use of MI systems in the OST field.

This monograph examines the use of MI systems by OST providers and city-level policymakers in eight case-study cities: the five Wallace initiative sites and three others (Denver, Louisville, and San Francisco). A companion monograph, *Hours of Opportunity*, Volume 1: *Lessons from Five Cities on Building Systems to Improve After-School, Summer School, and Other Out-of-School-Time Programs* (Bodily et al., 2010), examines the system-building efforts of the Wallace initiative sites. A third RAND publication, *Hours of Opportunity*, Volume 3: *Profiles of Five Cities Improving After-School Programs Through a Systems Approach* (McCombs et al., 2010), presents case studies of the Wallace-funded cities' system-building efforts, including the development and implementation of MI systems.

While there is substantial literature on the use of MI systems in the private sector and data-based decisionmaking in the private and education sectors, few studies examine how MI systems support decisionmaking in the OST sector. A few factors have contributed to the OST sector's relatively late adoption of these methods and technologies. Namely, the sector is characterized by limited funds for large capital expenditures, low levels of provider familiarity with such systems, and a high level of fragmentation.

This monograph presents insights from eight cities and is structured around three overarching research questions:

1. Why and how were MI systems for OST adopted in citywide efforts?
2. How are city MI systems currently used and implemented by various stakeholders?
   - What is the status of implementation in each of the cities?
   - What do cities do to ensure data quality?
   - How and to what extent do city-level officials and providers use data from MI systems?
3. What factors have enabled or hindered implementation?

Concepts Behind the Study

The OST field is fraught with information asymmetry. Stakeholders frequently lack the information needed to make optimal decisions. Making optimal decisions requires a transfer of information among stakeholders. For instance, a city agency or intermediary funding OST programs needs to decide which providers to fund, where to place programs, and which groups of children or youth to target with its resources. The funder has knowledge of the amount of funding it has and the interests of the city. However, to make the best decisions about how to target resources, the funder needs additional information that describes the content and quality of programming; the capacity of providers; the history of participation in programs; the location of OST programs across the city; the needs, desires, and concerns of parents and youth; and the overall interests of the community. These data are held by various other stakeholders in the OST system.

Information Collection and Sharing

A review of the literature and earlier RAND research provided some ideas about the type of information that needs to be analyzed and interpreted to enable optimal decisionmaking among the various stakeholders involved in citywide OST programming (see Table 1.1).

Table 1.1
General Decisions and Information in a Possible OST System

Affiliation	Decisions	Information Owned	Information Needs
City agency or intermediary	Which program to fund Where to fund programs Which populations to target	Available funds Interest of city leaders Demographics of city	Content of programming Quality of programming Capacity of provider organizations Students served by OST programs Frequency of student attendance Needs, desires, and concerns of parents/youth Interests of community
School	Whether to offer programs to students Which programs to offer to students	Student demographics Student performance Student needs	Needs, desires, and concerns of parents/youth Content of programming Quality of programming Capacity of provider organizations Students served by programs
Provider	Which programs to provide Where to provide programs Which populations to target How to improve programs	Content of programs Quality of programs Attendance in programs Populations served	Needs, desires, and concerns of parents/youth Student outcomes
Parent/youth	Whether to enroll in programs Which programs to select	Interests Needs Concerns Satisfaction	Location of programs Quality of programming

The concept of an OST system in which these stakeholders effectively coordinate to benefit children implies the creation of data-sharing mechanisms so that important information is transferred. Cities might use a number of mechanisms to collect and disseminate data. An OST MI system that collects program information and tracks participant enrollment, attendance, and outcomes is just one mechanism. Others include the following:

- *market research*, which involves gathering information on the needs, interests, and concerns of youth, parents, and community members to understand access, demand, and perceived quality
- *program locators*, typically searchable websites, which provide information about the location and content of programs to parents and youth
- *memoranda of understanding* between organizations that allow for the sharing of data on youth (for instance, a memorandum of understanding between the public school system and a city agency to share student data)
- *data bridges*, or joint MI platforms that allow the direct transfer of information from one MI system to another (for instance, to directly link a public school MI system to an OST MI system to allow providers to immediately access information such as student identification numbers, demographic data, attendance, grades, and test scores)
- *quality assessments*, which gather standardized information about the quality of programs.

While an OST MI system is only one among many mechanisms that can be used by groups of organizations to support information sharing, it is a powerful one. Data from OST MI systems can inform city funding decisions, targeting of professional development resources, and programming choices, and it can signal potential quality problems, by using enrollment and attendance as rough quality indicators. Information from MI systems can also be provided to other stakeholders. For instance, information about the content and location of programs can be compiled and shared with parents and youth.

Factors Influencing Management Information System Implementation and Use of Data

Simply purchasing computers and software for data collection will not lead to data-based decisionmaking (Schoech, 1995; Kagle, 1993). For an MI system to be used to support improvements in an OST system, (1) providers must enter timely and accurate information into the MI system, (2) stakeholders (city agencies, intermediaries, and providers) must analyze (or hire an evaluator to analyze) the data and then report the results to decisionmakers, and (3) decisionmakers must act on the data. Decisionmakers include a variety of actors, such as mayors, city council members, agency heads, private funders, superintendents, principals, and executive directors of CBOs providing OST services. As described earlier, data-based decisions can lead to better OST provision and improved outcomes for participants. In addition, the use of data can generate clearer views of which data are needed, leading to alterations in data-collection activities. Prior research suggests a number of facilitators and obstacles to these steps.

First, the importance of timely, accurate, and complete data should not be underestimated, because these characteristics will influence how stakeholders use the data. A number of factors influence the quality of the data in the MI system. Leadership in the provider organization as well as staff buy-in regarding the MI system and its broader goals can influence the accuracy of the data (Carrilio, 2005; Botcheva, White, and Huffman, 2002). Staff who do not understand why the data are collected may see data entry as an unimportant administrative task that can be put off or completed inaccurately without harming the organization or its goals. Also, because of the potential to affect an organization's funding and future, there can be disincentives to using systems that collect data about program performance. Leaders must believe that the collection and use of data are in their own and the agency's best interest, rather than an interference to the "real" work of the organization (Hasenfeld and Patti, 1992; Carrilio, 2005). In addition, the match between the data collected and defined program and systemic goals will influence the extent to which the data will inform decisionmaking.

Training on the system is vital. In a field in which computer knowledge is uneven and staff turnover is high, providing ongoing opportunities for training is vital (Herrera and Arbreton, 2003; Carrilio, 2005). Even the most user-friendly MI system requires training and a period of learning (Barrett, 1999; Fitzgerald and Murphy, 1994). The usability of the system, users' comfort with technology, and the responsiveness of the MI system (which depends on networks and servers) will influence the use of the system and the validity of the data entered into it (Visscher and Bloemen, 1999). High-quality training and technical assistance can also positively influence timely and accurate data entry (Goodhue, 1995; Rocheleau, 2000).

Second, a variety of factors can facilitate or inhibit the analysis and use of data. How the MI system is developed and introduced, including the rationale for the system, the information collected, and the logic model for its use, can affect the ability of city officials and providers to analyze and disseminate its data. Prior studies show that an organization must accurately assess its capacity to collect and analyze data (deAlwis, Majid, and Chaudhry, 2006; Mintzberg, 1978). The capacity of the personnel who analyze the data, including their analytic skills and the amount of time they can dedicate to this task, will influence the quality and utility of the analyses. Demand for analytic data from leaders can help improve capacity, for example, by providing staff with the time they need for analysis. Because providers are unlikely to have trained data analysts, creating ways for the MI system to generate useful reports is vital to ensuring that providers can make decisions based on these data (Breiter and Light, 2006).

Third, stakeholders must be able to make decisions that are informed by analysis of the data. Research on data-based decision-making in the education sector suggests that, while educators appreciate data (Hamilton et al., 2007; Kerr et al., 2006), they do not always know how to use that information effectively (Choppin, 2002; Feldman and Tung, 2001; Marsh, Pane, and Hamilton, 2006; Mason, 2002; Supovitz and Klein, 2003). Thus, having a defined process for using the data improves the probability that they will inform decisions. Further, the quality-management and accountability orientation of an organization will influence its ability to make use of data; simply purchasing computers and software for data collection will not lead to data-based decisions (Schoech, 1995; Kagle, 1993).

In summary, the theory is that using data from MI systems in decisionmaking could lead to improved OST services and improved access to programming for children and youth, which could, in turn, lead to better outcomes for participants. However, the factors described here can influence whether this vision is realized. These considerations guided our data-collection activities and analyses, described next.

Data and Methodology

We used a descriptive case analysis of eight major U.S. cities to investigate issues around OST MI system adoption, focusing on the use of such systems at the city and provider levels. In each of the case-study cities, we collected interview and survey data to create a picture of the implementation and use of MI systems by the major stakeholders.

Site Selection

Because the research described in this monograph was conducted as part of a larger study investigating The Wallace Foundation initiative, we included the five Wallace-funded cities: Boston, Chicago, New York City, Providence, and Washington, D.C. The Wallace Foundation was also interested in examining other cities to gain a broader understanding of city adoption of MI system for OST programming. The additional cities were not selected to serve as contrasts or comparisons for the Wallace initiative cities. We identified eight candidates through a literature review and interviews with officials from National League of Cities and representatives from MI system vendors. We conducted brief interviews with a lead contact from the candidate cities to ask about the proportion of city-funded providers using the MI system and uses of the MI system data. We then selected four of the cities in consultation with Wallace Foundation staff; three agreed to participate in the study: Denver, Louisville, and San Francisco.

Several factors influenced the selection of these cities. The first was geography. The majority of Wallace-funded sites were located on the East Coast, and The Foundation was interested in achieving geographical balance in the final sample. As a result, we did not add any East Coast cities to our study. We also considered how the cities used their MI systems and tried to include cities that used a variety of MI vendors. Finally, to reduce the research burden on cities, we avoided inviting smaller cities that were already participating in another Wallace-funded study regarding the participation of middle school youth in OST programs.

Collectively, the eight cities in the study provide illustrative examples of cities' development and implementation of MI systems to improve OST provision. However, they are not representative of all cities that have adopted MI systems to track OST programs.

Data Collection and Analysis

City Interviews. Teams of two to four RAND researchers conducted site visits in all eight cities and interviewed key stakeholders. We interviewed a range of city representatives, including leaders from agencies and intermediaries involved in funding OST programs and representatives of the mayor's office, the school district, schools, and provider organizations. Across the eight sites, we conducted 168 interviews. We used semistructured protocols that were guided by the themes we had identified from the literature that might affect the implementation and use of MI systems. However, the nature of our interviews varied depending on whether the city was part of the Wallace initiative. We visited the Wallace initiative cities in the spring of 2008 and 2009 and conducted a large number of interviews that focused on a range of activities, of which the adoption of an MI system was just one. In the cities that were not part of the Wallace initiative, we interviewed fewer people but focused solely on questions about the MI system. These visits were conducted in fall 2008. Table 1.2 presents the number of interviewees by site and type of respondent in each city.

The RAND researchers used typed notes and digital recordings of the interviews to create a complete record of each interview. To analyze these interview data, we created descriptive site case write-ups by summarizing evidence that appeared in the interview records concerning each of the following areas identified by the literature as

Table 1.2
Number of Site Interviews, by Type

Affiliation	Boston	Chicago	Denver	Louisville	New York City	Providence	San Francisco	Washington, D.C.	Total
Mayor's office	1	0	2	0	2	2	0	4	11
City agencies	4	10	0	5	9	9	2	1	40
District and schools	8	4	3	5	2	2	3	5	32
Intermediary organizations	7	0	0	0	4	4	0	8	23
OST providers	4	7	8	8	7	7	5	4	50
Evaluators	0	0	1	0	1	0	0	0	2
Funders	0	0	1	2	2	2	0	3	10
Total	24	21	15	20	27	26	10	25	168

important: the development process, training, data quality, data linkages and sharing, data use, and perceived benefits and challenges of implementation. In developing the case studies, we took care to examine interviewees' responses for consistency across individuals. Cases in which we found disagreement among respondents were noted. The descriptive cases were sent to leaders in each of the cities for fact-checking.

Finally, we examined the set of case summaries to develop the cross-case themes and findings that are presented in this monograph. We looked for similarities and differences across the sites and for consistent relationships among activities and reported outcomes. For instance, we examined whether there was a consistent relationship between training on the MI system and its use.

Vendor Interviews. During the summer of 2009, researchers conducted 45-minute telephone interviews with the leaders of five companies that are the major providers of MI systems for the OST sector: Cayen, Cityspan, EZ Reports, nFocus, and Social Solutions. While only three of these firms were vendors for cities in our study, each vendor served cities, states, school districts, and/or providers. Vendors provided important background information about the development of this field, their range of services, and their opinions regarding the future of MI systems in the OST sector. This information helped the research team better understand the context of MI system use in the sector.

Survey of Providers. Much of MI system effectiveness hinges on providers' use of and commitment to the MI system, so obtaining a full understanding of how providers use the system and the factors that help or hinder effective use was critical to the study. Due to the large number of providers in many cities, a survey was needed to obtain such information.

We developed and administered a 20-minute survey that covered the following topics and constructs drawn from the literature and thus aligned with our qualitative data collection. Topics on the survey included frequency of data entry, MI system training and support, leadership, buy-in, usability of the system, use of data, usefulness of data, and perceived validity of the collected data. We also asked for descriptive program data (e.g., number of children served, grade level of children served, the focus of the program). Survey respondents tended to be executive directors, OST program managers (i.e., those in charge of one or multiple OST programs), or site coordinators (i.e., individuals in charge of coordinating multiple OST program offerings at a school).

The number of OST providers that were using each city's MI system varied widely. For instance, Denver listed 12 providers, while New York City listed 625 providers. In Boston, the survey was not applicable because the new MI system was still in development during the survey administration period. In each city surveyed except New York City, we surveyed the entire list of providers we were given.[1] For New York City, we drew a random sample of 225 programs. The survey was administered from January through March 2009. As shown in Table 1.3, we surveyed a total of 524 programs and received responses from 358, for an overall response rate of 68 percent. City-level response rates varied from 93 percent in Denver to 58 percent in Chicago. Additional details regarding survey administration, sampling, and weighting can be found in the appendix.

We conducted site-specific basic tabulations and used factor analysis to identify scales around certain constructs from our survey data (e.g., perceived usefulness of data). We also ran regression analyses to examine correlations between various predictors and the perceived usefulness of MI system data.[2]

---

[1]   Note that, for Washington, D.C., we were provided with contact information for providers that were part of the Project My Time initiative, funded by The Wallace foundation, and not all programs using the DC Children and Youth Investment Trust Corporation's MI system. For Chicago, we were provided with a list of OST programs funded by Family and Support Services (FSS) but not programs funded by the Chicago Public Schools (CPS) or the Chicago Park District, which were also using an MI system. In San Francisco, we focused on and surveyed providers using the Department of Children, Youth, and Their Families (DCYF) MI system. In Boston, we were unable to conduct a survey because the new MI system was still in development.

[2]   To conduct this simple regression model, we used Proc Survey Reg in SAS, with site-specific dummy variables to control for differences in the size of our sites.

Table 1.3
Survey Response Rates

Site	Number Contacted	Number Responding	Response Rate (%)
Chicago	139	81	58
Washington, D.C.	18	15	83
Denver	14	13	93
Louisville	25	21	84
Providence	19	15	79
New York City	183	126	69
San Francisco	126	87	69
Total/average	524	358	68

Study Limitations

This study was based on eight cases of city adoption of MI systems for OST, and while the cases provide important examples, they are not intended to be representative all U.S. cities' efforts, nor should they be considered "exemplars" of MI system implementation. Moreover, this study focused on the adoption and use of cities' MI systems. Many providers have their own MI systems for tracking programming and outcomes. In particular, many large, national providers (e.g., Boys and Girls Club) have been using their own MI systems independent of city efforts to spread use among providers.

Further, the scope of this research did not include collecting detailed information about costs. For details about the cost of MI systems, see Hayes et al., 2009. Nor did the study focus on the technical aspects of MI systems hardware and software.

The study relied on self-reported data from a sample of participants and is subject to common potential biases associated with such data. In addition, there was unevenness in our data collection. Some cities had adopted their systems several years prior to data collection, so information about adoption rationale and challenges in these cities was far less detailed and may be less accurate than in cities that more recently adopted a MI system. Also, the content and scope of our interviews differed in Wallace initiative and non–Wallace initiative cities.

Finally, this monograph covers accomplishments up to spring 2009. Work around MI systems has continued in the cities; thus, by publication, activities in theses cities may have evolved beyond what is presented here.

Despite these limitations, this descriptive analysis provides important information about the implementation of MI systems from the city and provider perspectives and will be helpful to other city leaders considering adopting such a system.

A Note on Terminology

In the main body of this monograph, we typically refer to each city as having an "MI system" rather than calling out the specific name of its system. We do this for two reasons. First, it eases the burden on the reader who will not have to retain the specific names (e.g. Youthservices.net, OST Online, Cityspan, KidTrax). Second, we want to avoid any perception we are promoting the use of one MI system over others. We did not evaluate these systems nor did we include cities using all of the possible MI systems available in the marketplace. However, in some cities, a reference to the "city" MI system is overly simplistic. Some cities (e.g., San Francisco) have multiple MI systems in use or in development by different youth-serving agencies. Overall, although simplification was necessary for the cross-case analysis, we do clarify the cities' contexts in Chapter Two.

Also, in this monograph (with the exception of the city context discussion in Chapter Two), we use generic terminology to describe city stakeholders to ease the burden on readers. City agencies and intermediaries are referred to as such rather than by their city-specific names.

We use the term *providers* to refer to respondents in CBOs that offer OST services to children and youth.

Organization of This Monograph

Chapter Two describes the cities' rationale for MI system adoption, decisions made in developing the systems, and how the MI systems were used as of spring 2009. Chapter Three explains how cities tried to ensure the quality of data entered into the systems. Chapter Four focuses on providers' experiences with city MI systems and how they use the data. Chapter Five concludes with lessons for other cities interested in adopting MI systems to support improved OST programming. The appendix provides technical details about survey sampling, administration, weighting procedures, and our statistical modeling of the survey results.

CHAPTER TWO

Cities' Development and Use of Out-of-School-Time Management Information Systems

Each of the cities in our study had a unique context, which resulted in differences in the goals for the MI system, the proportion of city-funded programs included, development decisions, and how the MI system and its data were ultimately used. We begin this chapter with discussion of the shared rationale for the investment in MI systems in the eight cities. We then provide a brief overview of the city context and the status of the MI system in each city (as of spring 2009), including its specific goals, scope, and stage of development. The chapter then discusses how city context influenced MI system development decisions in each of the cities. Finally, we describe how cities reported using data from the MI systems. Throughout the chapter, we highlight specific examples from the cities and note the variety of approaches taken.

Shared Goals for Management Information Systems

Interviewees in the eight cities mentioned a number of reasons for investing in an MI system. First and foremost, they expressed a desire to gather accurate data on programs and participants. Prior to implementing an MI system, city agencies and intermediaries lacked very basic information, such as which providers were being funded, how many children and youth were served by programs, the characteristics of participants, and attendance. Further, the data they did have were considered highly inaccurate. In fact, we were told by city interviewees and vendors that, when agencies and intermediaries switched to collecting enrollment and attendance data through an MI system, the number of students they thought they were serving sometimes dropped by a third. All the leaders in the eight cities considered lower, accurate data to be far more beneficial than inflated, inaccurate counts.

City Context and the Goals of the Cities' Management Information Systems

The cities in our study varied in terms of size, goals for the MI system, source of funding for the MI system, the agency responsible for the MI system, and whether they had more than one MI system (see Table 2.1). These city contexts resulted in differences in the proportion of city-funded programs the MI system tracked. Here, we provide a brief overview of these factors as a basis for the remainder of this monograph. This information was current as of spring 2009 but may be out of date because MI system development was ongoing in many of the cities.

Boston

Boston received a grant from The Wallace Foundation in 2006 to support OST system-building efforts. The intermediary that was leading the work under the grant (Boston After School and Beyond) adopted an MI system for ten demonstration schools. In 2008, responsibility for implementation under the grant was transferred to a division of the Boston Public Schools (the Department of Extended Learning Time, Afterschool, and Services, or DELTAS), and Boston's Wallace initiative expanded to cover a larger set of schools (42 total) that shared a similar after-school model. Use of the first MI system was discontinued in the demonstration schools. DELTAS decided to develop its own MI system (DELTAS MIS) with automatic links to the Boston Public Schools data system, because a key goal was to actively link after-school programs to the school day. Respondents described wanting to use these linked data to better understand the system of support provided to students, which would allow after-school providers to actively target specific services to specific youth based on individual needs and to target nonparticipating

Table 2.1
City Context and Scope of Management Information Systems as of Spring 2009

Site (MI system implementation date)	City Context	Lead Agency	Scope	In-House Development or External Vendor?	Contract Mgmt?	Automatic Link to Other Systems?	Multiple City MI Systems?
Boston (2006, 2009)	An intermediary was selected to lead Wallace initiative activities then transferred to lead role to an office in the district (DELTAS); DELTAS supports some after-school program provision in certain schools (Triumph Collaborative); city funds OST through city agency responsible for community centers	Intermediary moved to school district	Intermediary implemented MI system in 10 demonstration schools (abandoned 2008) Triumph Collaborative schools (42) will operate new MI system developed by district office	External system replaced by an internally developed system	No	Yes (district MI system)	Yes, city agency developing MI system (2008–2009)
Chicago (2006)	Multiple, strong city agencies funding large numbers of OST programs; strong, nationally recognized intermediary	Three city agencies (FSS, CPS, Parks District) and intermediary (After School Matters)	Three city agencies and intermediary each have an MI system that collects a common set of data (820+ programs, majority but not all)	External	Yes	No	Yes, but data can be easily merged

Table 2.1—Continued

Site (MI system implementation date)	City Context	Lead Agency	Scope	In-House Development or External Vendor?	Contract Mgmt?	Automatic Link to Other Systems?	Multiple City MI Systems?
Denver (2006)	Strong interest in coordination and new LOAS initiative; city funds large number of programs but lacks resources for system building	City agency (Mayor's Office for Education and Children)	12 schools in longitudinal evaluation; desire to move beyond pilot schools	External	No	No	No
Louisville (2002)	Strong existing collaboration between school district and city funding agency providing small grants to moderate number of providers	City agency and school district	67 OST programs (not all funded programs)	External	No	Yes	No
New York City (2006)	Newly consolidated funding into city agency (DYCD), which funded a large number of programs	City agency (DYCD)	DYCD-funded OST programs (625); 2009 addition of Beacon middle school programs	In-house	Yes	No	No

Table 2.1—Continued

Site (MI system implementation date)	City Context	Lead Agency	Scope	In-House Development or External Vendor?	Contract Mgmt?	Automatic Link to Other Systems?	Multiple City MI Systems?
Providence (2005)	No city agency responsible for OST; intermediary (PASA) created to lead OST work	Intermediary (PASA)	All programming in five middle school AfterZones; 22 providers and partners had a license to use the tracking system, including the four site-management agencies, all 10 recreation centers, and several CBOs	External	No	No	No
San Francisco (1998)	City agency funding OST programs (DCYF) since 2005; press for greater coordination among OST supporting agencies	City agency (DCYF)	DCYF-funded OST programs (150)	External	Yes	No	3 other city MI systems
Washington, D.C. (2002)	City provides intermediary (the Trust) funds to support OST contracts; new role of District of Columbia Public Schools supporting OST provision	Intermediary (the Trust)	Trust-funded programs (59)	External	Yes	No	As of 2008–2009, schools used DC STARS

students for recruitment into programs. As one interviewee in Boston described the MI system,

> [It] promises to be a whole-school tool. It is more than just attendance tracking; it is a whole-school approach—connecting OST to outcomes. We can see how after-school participation relates to attendance, which connects to GPA [grade point average]. We also want it to connect to referrals. If Malik is having a bad day, and I find out that he has had a death in the family, I can refer him to someone else, and the DELTAS MIS will have that information and will send out a reminder to follow up about that referral.

Concurrently, in 2008, a city agency responsible for Boston's community centers (Boston Centers for Youth and Families) contracted to implement yet a third MI system in its community centers.

Chicago

Chicago received a Wallace implementation grant in 2006 and focused its early efforts primarily on developing MI systems for the three leading city agencies that funded OST provision—FSS, CPS, and the Chicago Park District—and After School Matters a nationally recognized OST provider that was a key partner in Chicago's system-building efforts. Each agency adopted its own MI system to meet its agency-specific needs; however, all the systems were developed by the same vendor and collected a core set of common data, so data from all these MI systems could easily be merged to provide an overall view of the city's OST provision. Chicago leaders considered MI system development a method of starting coordination efforts among independent, youth-serving agencies. The theory was that, by working jointly on this effort and collecting common data, it would increase the demand for future coordination. As of 2009, more than 820 providers in Chicago were using a city-supported MI system.

Denver

Denver was not a Wallace grantee; however, the city was working to improve coordination and collaboration around OST provision. In

2003, Denver launched its Lights on After School (LOAS) initiative as a collaborative effort among the Denver Public School Foundation, the Mayor's Office for Education and Children, and the Mile High United Way. LOAS offered funding and program support to after-school programs in Denver's elementary and middle schools. In 2006, Denver adopted an MI system for programs operating in 12 schools to provide data for a longitudinal evaluation to track the effects of OST on a variety of participant outcomes. The goal of the evaluation was to provide information that could be used to improve the more than 700 city-funded OST programs in Denver. In addition, the school district downloaded a subset of data into the MI system on a regular basis, creating a link between OST and the school day. Denver leaders said that they wanted to have more providers and schools use the MI system, but a lack of resources constrained expansion.

Louisville

Louisville was not a Wallace initiative grantee; however, the city's main OST funding agency (the Louisville Metro Office of Youth Development) had been working closely with the school district (Jefferson County Public Schools) on OST issues for almost a decade. Leaders in Louisville viewed the MI system as a method for continuing an already existing collaboration between the public school system and the city's main OST funding agency. In 2002, the two partners adopted an MI system for use by the city funding agency grantees. A data bridge linked the OST MI system to a set of district data that included student information, such as district ID number, address, birth date, school attendance record, grades, and state test scores. All provider organizations and MI system users in that organization signed a confidentiality agreement to access the data bridge system. City officials noted that the small number of providers in the community and the high level of trust among the stakeholders facilitated giving OST providers access to district data. City officials envisioned that providers would use the MI system to make programmatic improvements to meet desired academic, behavioral, and socioemotional outcomes. All providers receiving $10,000 or more from the Office of Youth Development were required to use the MI system, and, in 2008, 67 provider organizations across 90 OST sites were using it.

New York City

New York City received a Wallace implementation grant in 2005. During the planning period for the grant, New York City consolidated into one agency (the Department of Youth and Community Development, or DYCD) much of the OST funding that had been spread among multiple city agencies. In 2006, DYCD rolled out its own MI system and mandated its use as part of a new contracting process. The desire to create an MI system aligned with the mayor's results-based approach to city management, and, in fact, he emphasized developing information technology (IT) capacity citywide. Leaders in DYCD viewed the MI system as a critical driver of better contract management, and participation data were directly linked to provider payments. In 2009, all DYCD-funded OST programs, approximately 625 providers, used the MI system and separately administered middle school programs, Beacon programs (school-based community centers) were going to start using the system.

Providence

Providence received a Wallace implementation grant in 2004. Providence did not have a city agency that funded OST programming. Thus, an intermediary (the Providence After School Alliance, or PASA) was created to lead Providence's OST system-building efforts. In 2005, the intermediary adopted an MI system to track participation and attendance among providers operating in all its middle school AfterZones, which hosted a number of after-school programs. One key motivation for adopting an MI system in Providence was that it would support daily management. In particular, it would allow site coordinators at the AfterZones to report on the location of each student participant in real time and help coordinate transportation home. During early planning for its system-building efforts, Providence learned that parents had concerns about student safety in after-school programs, so leaders viewed a data system that could report student location and help manage transportation home as a method to increase youth participation in OST programs.

San Francisco

San Francisco was not a Wallace grantee; however, in 2005, the mayor and superintendent initiated a citywide after-school coordination effort, the Afterschool for All initiative. San Francisco's use of an MI system predates this initiative. In 1998, a city agency (DCYF) began using an MI system with its grantees to support better contract management. In 1999, it required all OST providers to use the MI system, and, in 2003, it expanded the scope of the data collected in order to support an external evaluation. Because the evaluation sought to link attendance and outcomes measured by pre- and postassessments, each provider was required to establish its own program goals and assessments to measure those goals and to enter those into the MI system. San Francisco leaders reported that the sheer volume and variety of programmatic outcomes made these data too difficult to manage and analyze. Recognizing that the department did not have the capacity to effectively use all the information collected and that grantees were struggling to meet all the data-reporting requirements, the outcome elements of the system were "decommissioned." The evaluation aspect was scaled back, and DCYF launched a new version of the MI system in 2004 based on feedback from providers.

As of 2009, more than 180 providers used this MI system. Three other OST-funding agencies in San Francisco also used their own MI systems. For the purposes of the study, we focused on the MI system adopted by DCYF because of the agency's the long history with it.

Washington, D.C.

Washington, D.C. received a Wallace implementation grant in 2006, which was given to an intermediary organization (DC Children and Youth Investment Trust Corporation, commonly referred to as the Trust). The Trust's adoption of an MI system predated The Wallace Foundation's funding; it had used an MI system to support better contract management since 2003. Approximately 60 programs used the MI system in 2009. In 2008, the school district began operating OST programs in each public school in the city and began tracking OST participation in its own school district database. The mayor frequently demanded data on OST participation from the Trust and the public schools to inform city-level decisionmaking. In 2009, the Trust issued a request for proposals (RFP) to develop a new MI system with different capabilities.

Overarching Development Decisions

When developing the systems described here, cities made a series of decisions. A few macro-level decisions regarding the development of the MI systems emerged during our conversations with city officials, which we describe next: selection of an in-house or external developer, whether to pilot the system, and whether to modify or replace an MI system.

Developer Decision

Each city in our study made decisions about whether to hire an outside vendor to develop and support its MI system or to develop it internally. Since the late 1990s, MI system vendors have developed software to track OST participation. In fact, at the time of the study, there were several firms that specialized in developing MI systems for the OST sector, including Cayen, Cityspan, EZ Reports, nFocus, and Social Solutions. These firms developed MI systems for cities, states, school districts, and provider organizations to track general OST, Supplemental Education Services, and summer job programs. While these vendors all had "off-the-shelf" products, they specialized in adapting software to suit unique needs and contexts. For instance, even within Chicago, the vendor developed four MI systems that were customized for the goals of the major organizations funding OST programming (see text box). MI system vendors provided a range of technical assistance and training and had the capability to use a variety of technological applications, such as card or fingerprint scanning, to help track attendance. In cities that decided to select an outside vendor, some agencies and

MI System Development in Chicago

The MI system vendor worked with the project director (who had extensive expertise in MI system development) and representatives from the partner agencies to design a system for each agency. Although many data-tracking functions were standardized across all the partner sites, the MI system vendor and the project director worked to provide customization for each partner according to its individual information needs. One key activity was for each agency to outline its goals and purpose so that data collection would match and support those agency objectives. For example, FSS, CPS, and After School Matters wanted the capability to post and collect RFPs and monitor budgets, stipends, and invoices. The Chicago Park District was not interested in adding these capabilities. Tracking hours of participation was another example of an area where city agencies differed. Some wanted the MI system to capture this information while others did not. The most customized and perhaps complex modifications were for After School Matters, which needed to track instructor and participant surveys, teen applications, instructor RFPs, and instructor payments and invoices. Chicago's planning practice aligns with the MI system literature, which stresses the importance of spending considerable time up front to understand what information will be most useful to the consumer (Breiter and Light, 2006).

intermediaries issued an RFP for the MI system and some reached out to other cities with MI systems for vendor recommendations.

Two of the eight cities in our study (New York City and Boston) determined that it was best to develop their own MI systems. In New York City, the lead OST agency worked with a software developer to build a custom system that was then supported by the city. The desire to create a customized MI system fit with the mayor's priorities and management style, which can be described as data-driven. Further, the mayor had placed an emphasis on developing information technology capacity citywide. In Boston, the district office supporting after-school programming decided to work with an individual developer to create an MI system that was directly linked to the main district server, which would allow an immediate link between OST data and school-day data. For these cities, the desire for full control over the system was paramount.

Each of these cities faced somewhat more challenging roll outs than the other cities. In New York City, the MI system needed several modifications before being considered highly functional by city officials and providers (as it was at the time of our data collection). However, the need for a very short development time frame contributed to this as well. New York City officials actively solicited input from providers and modified the system to help meet their needs. In Boston, implementation and use of the MI system was stalled because of limited server capacity in the district system.

Method of Management Information System Introduction

Each city launched its MI system in a way that reflected its context and constraints. Many cities did not feel the need to conduct an elaborate pilot test of the system before full implementation by all providers. On the other hand, in Chicago, one of the agencies conducted a pilot in part because leaders felt that the process could help build buy-in among the provider community. The city also gave a computer to each provider participating in the pilot. Leaders in Chicago believed this strategy paid off and resulted in improved buy-in from the provider community upon full implementation. Indeed, in response to the open-ended question on the survey, one provider wrote,

> As part of the [MI system] Pilot Project, I appreciated the opportunity to provide feedback/input about the MI system program, and I was pleased and satisfied when recommendations were implemented. . . .

New York City's OST agency was unable to pilot its new MI system due to timing constraints. The funding agency implementing the system was initiating an entirely new system of contracting for OST that required providers to use the MI system. Because the agency needed to implement its MI system in September 2006 (when the first round of new OST programs started), there was no pilot test of the system before 550 programs began using it. We were told that the rollout was "very rocky," which was not surprising given the short development time frame. However, New York City officials thought that the benefit of having the entire system start on time outweighed the cost of not having a pilot.

Changes to and Replacement of Management Information Systems

MI systems evolve over time, and cities described adding capabilities, changing the types of data gathered, and working to improve their systems to make them more user-friendly. For instance, in New York City, fields were added and modified based on feedback from providers and city agency staff. In response to provider requests, the city agency allowed providers to enter data for children they served who were not funded by the city. In Providence, city leaders added the capacity to process RFPs in their MI system and to track budgets. In San Francisco, the city agency scaled back on the data initially collected to reduce the burden on providers.

Changing context in two cities led to the adoption of new MI systems. In Boston, the system-building work started with an intermediary. The intermediary had selected an MI system vendor for its ten demonstration schools, based in part on the belief that the school district would be adopting this system to track participation in Supplemental Education Services; however, the district did not adopt this system. When responsibility for the work of The Wallace Foundation grant transferred to an office in the school district, the district decided that it wanted the OST MI system to link directly to school-day data. Thus, the demonstration sites discontinued use of the initial MI system, and the school district built its own MI system that was linked to the school district database.

In Washington, D.C., the local intermediary adopted an MI system for contract management years before the Wallace initiative. Because the intermediary changed how it wanted to use the MI system and its data—moving beyond contract management to include expanded quality management—it contracted to build a new MI system in the spring of 2009. The intermediary's RFP asked for an MI system with the following functions: the ability to track individual students across funded programs, the use of scan-card technology to track attendance, and measurement of program outcomes through participant assessments and surveys. It also expressed a preference that the MI system allow providers to build customized participant-level data fields accessible only to that provider.

Cities' Use of Data from the Management Information System

Through analysis of interview data, we identified seven distinct uses of MI system data: (1) understanding and improving programming and participation, (2) improving OST contract management, (3) making funding decisions, (4) changing the nature of contract management to focus on quality, (5) improving coordination through data sharing, (6) informing evaluations, and (7) supporting requests for continued or additional funding. We discuss these uses in turn, highlighting specific examples from the cities and noting the variety of approaches taken. We also discuss the enablers and constraints of MI system use as described by respondents.

Understanding and Improving Programming and Participation

The cities cited a variety of uses for MI system data (see Table 2.2), but first and foremost, all of them used these data to better understand OST programming and participation (e.g., enrollment, attendance, demographics). The importance of this use cannot be underestimated. Prior to MI system adoption, the cities could say little about the programs they funded or the youth being served. As one interviewee put it,

> The biggest benefit is knowing what we are buying with these programs because, for so many years, we worked off our projections and aggregate numbers provided by CBOs. When we went to real data, our numbers dropped to like 40,000 kids. The benefit has been that now we know who we are reaching, how often, and how much money we are spending.

Table 2.2
Cities' Use of Data from OST Management Information Systems

Use	Chicago (2006)	Denver (2006)	Louisville (2002)	New York City (2006)	Providence (2005)	San Francisco (1998)	Washington, D.C. (2002)
Understanding and improving programming and participation	X	X	X	X	X	X	X
Improving OST contract management	X		X	X	X	X	X
Making funding decisions				X	X		
Changing the nature of contract management to focus on quality	X			X	X	X	
Improving coordination through data sharing	X	X	X	X	X		
Informing evaluations		X	X	X	X	X	
Supporting requests for continued or additional funding		X	X	X	X		

NOTE: The date of MI system implementation is listed under each city's name. An "X" indicates that more than one respondent described the given use of data.

By design, in some cities, MI system adoption was extensive among the population of providers, and a significant percentage of city-funded OST participation was being tracked (e.g., New York City, Chicago), whereas in other sites, adoption was rather modest and captured a small share of OST participation (e.g., Denver).

City agencies and intermediaries also used these data to track programming and participation in unique ways. For instance, as described earlier, the intermediary in Providence used the MI system to organize transportation for OST participants. It also used attendance reports to follow up with students who were absent and used data to help OST providers structure their programs to best serve the needs and interests of their target populations.

Funding partners in Denver used MI system participation data to identify population groups prone to dropping out of OST programs. Funders determined that middle school students were particularly likely to drop out of programming. Subsequently, the LOAS partnership worked with OST site coordinators to design programs that would better engage this age group. Similarly, in Chicago, the school district and park district both cited examples of using participant characteristics and participation rates to inform programming decisions. For example, if 75 percent of after-school participants were girls, a school might change its programming to attract more boys. The mayor's office in Washington, D.C., used the intermediary's MI system data to map the concentration of OST services provided across the city and push for greater coverage, especially in areas where there were large numbers of high-need youth.

Improving OST Contract Management

Agency and intermediary leaders in New York City, Chicago, Washington, D.C., and San Francisco all reported that they used their MI systems to improve contract management. For instance, the funding agency in San Francisco used the MI system to manage contracts with grant recipients and to remit payments through a monthly invoicing feature. In fact, the agency has set up the system to remit payments only if enrollment and attendance targets are met. The funding agency in New York City monitored contractual compliance by regularly examining information entered into its MI system. In fact, the agency directly linked payment of providers to their ability to meet attendance targets. Similarly, in Washington, D.C., the intermediary used its MI system to regularly review enrollment and attendance data and to identify and remedy problems. It issued payments only after receiving quarterly reports, and sometimes adjustments were made based on enrollment and attendance. In Chicago, three major OST funders (FSS, Afterschool Matters, and CPS) posted and collected responses to RFPs through their MI systems, and each reported using its MI system to monitor budgets and invoices.

Making Funding Decisions

Two cities described making funding decisions based on the data. In Providence, city managers used past enrollment reports as one source of information during funding review meetings. New York City formally used the MI system as a basis for provider compensation. Providers in New York City entered descriptions of services they planned to provide into the MI system, which were reviewed by the funding agency for approval or rejection. These descriptions then became the contract under which the agency held each provider accountable. Using the MI system and a contract management data system, the agency evaluated provider performance and reduced funding for providers that did not meet attendance targets. The agency also used MI system data to direct additional funding to select successful programs (as measured by attendance). We were told that using data to make decisions that align with the agency's vision also helped the agency stand by those decisions, even when they resulted in a loss of funding for a provider. As one respondent noted, the agency can say, "Based on the data that we have before us, these are the right decisions."

Changing the Nature of Contract Management

Interviewees in New York City and Chicago told us that the collection and use of data shifted the nature of contract management. According to respondents, prior to implementation of an MI system, the management of OST providers was being strictly contractual and focused on "paper" rather than programs. In both these cities, managers in the city agencies described using the MI system to generate reports of average daily attendance for providers on a periodic basis. If attendance rates dropped below certain levels, managers followed up with providers to determine whether there were problems that needed to be addressed. In this way, declining attendance served as a red flag for potential quality problems. In New York City, struggling providers received referrals for additional professional development at no cost to the provider. Respondents in New York City and Chicago noted that the MI system allowed them to detect problems in OST programs earlier, more efficiently, and across a larger number of programs than before.

In Providence, the intermediary checked attendance data from the MI system on an almost-daily basis and used it as a signal of possible quality problems. Staff members from the intermediary reported visiting programs that might be struggling almost immediately in order to assess whether the provider needed assistance, which may have been facilitated by Providence's relatively small size.

While the funding agency in San Francisco did not use attendance data to guide quality intervention, it was beginning to provide performance information to every provider. Starting in 2008, the agency created an end-of-year report for every program. The report included projected and actual average daily attendance broken down by age, racial/ethnic group, and summer or school-year period. Agency officials told us that these reports were reviewed with program officers in the agency who monitored the providers to determine whether the data were an accurate reflection of the programs and whether there were discrepancies. Once the reports were reviewed by the city agency, they were sent to providers for review and discussion.

Improving Coordination Through Data Sharing

Cities reported that the creation and use of MI systems improved coordination among city organizations. We found a wide range of OST data-sharing agreements across the study sites. Some cities shared MI system reports with various stakeholders but did not link the MI system to other data systems. For instance, in New York City, the main funding agency shared OST participation information with another agency serving younger children (the Administration for Child Services). This data sharing allowed the two agencies to track and understand continuation of services for eligible children from early childhood through their school years. Data were also shared with the city's department of education.

In Chicago, one of the key goals of the MI system was to improve coordination among the four major city funders of OST programming. The theory was that the data would encourage conversations among the agencies. During the initial years of implementation, each agency had access to data pertaining to its own programs. In 2009, Chicago produced its first merged data file to which all agencies had access, and agency representatives were convened to discuss the data.

In Providence, reports from the MI system were regularly shared at meetings with stakeholders responsible for overseeing the OST effort (e.g., the PASA board).

Other cities established agreements to link the MI system to school outcomes to permit an evaluation of the relationship between OST participation and children and youth outcomes. MI system data were linked to school district data in Providence, Louisville, and Denver. Similarly, several agencies in Washington, D.C., including the intermediary, agreed to participate in data sharing to link school district, OST participation, and health and human services data.

Informing Evaluations

MI system data supported evaluations conducted in the cities. For instance, a number of cities used MI system data to examine the links and correlations between OST participation and a variety of student outcomes. Since 2002, Denver had commissioned annual studies to examine the effect of OST programming on student outcomes, such as attendance and achievement (see text box). Similarly, in Louisville, several studies conducted by the school district found positive associations between program participation and academic outcomes. New York City's external evaluator drew on MI system data, and Providence's external evaluator used MI system participation data in its outcome study. In Chicago, the school district linked its OST MI system data with school data to look for associations between OST program participation and test scores and behavior. Sources said that the results of

---

External Evaluation in Denver

Denver used MI system data to evaluate and publicize its OST programming efforts. Beginning with the 2002–2003 school year, the Denver Public Schools commissioned an annual evaluation of OST programs and their association with outcomes such as student achievement and school attendance. Early evaluations examined six comprehensive program sites, expanded to include 11 comprehensive sites in the 2006–2007 school year. The evaluators found that participation was positively related to achievement on state assessments. The evaluation also examined student persistence in OST programming. Almost half of students who attended OST programs in 2005–2006 returned the following year. The 2007–2008 evaluation was to examine the relationship between OST participation and high school dropout and graduation rates. City leaders developed briefing papers based on the evaluation results and used them in efforts to promote OST among principals, teachers, the school board, city leaders, and funders.

---

these analyses were used to lobby principals to support OST activities at their schools, because the results demonstrated positive associations between student achievement and OST participation.

Supporting Requests for Funding

Some agencies and intermediaries reported using MI system data to justify petitions for continued or additional funding. In Providence, the intermediary presented MI system reports to PASA's board of directors, city departments, and funders and used the reports to raise support for city OST efforts. In Denver, the public schools and other funding partners used results from annual evaluations conducted by an independent evaluator, which showed a positive relationship between OST participation and school outcomes, to highlight the importance of increasing investment in the city's youth services. In New York City, the main funding agency reported using MI system information on programming and students served to support bids for increased funding from the city. In fact, the agency's OST budget grew from $46.6 million in fiscal year (FY) 2006 to $118.2 million in FY 2009. As one respondent noted,

Our agency competes for dollars against other social service agencies. Because our agency has data that demonstrate the programs that are funded and the students that are served, our agency holds a competitive advantage above others.

Enablers and Constraints to the Use of Data from the Management Information System

Our comparative analysis of the study sites found a number of important enabling and constraining factors relevant to the effective use of MI systems. The following list is not exhaustive, but it highlights the most prominent issues that emerged in multiple cities.

Lack of resources constrained data collection and use. The Wallace Foundation initiative cities did not face a lack of funding because The Foundation's funding paid for MI system development. However, a couple of the non-Wallace cities reported facing funding constraints that limited the scope of their MI systems and use of system data. In Denver, the MI system was limited to 12 pilot sites that were part of the intense evaluation. Although city leaders expressed a desire to adopt the MI system for all city-funded programming, they noted that resources did not exist to support this expansion. In addition, many city agencies and intermediaries lacked the time and staff needed to conduct the type of data analysis they envisioned. Resources in these agencies and intermediaries tended to be limited, with staff facing many duties and demands on their time. For instance, in Louisville, funding agency officials expressed a desire to do more with the MI system data, but staffing constraints limited the ability to conduct additional analyses. Budget cuts due to the nationwide economic downturn caused a further reduction in this agency's staff resources. As one Louisville respondent noted, "We lack the resources to take [our work] to the next level."

Mayoral demand for data fueled its analysis and use. Mayoral demand seemed to provide a needed incentive for agencies to prioritize the generation of reports and analyses of MI system data. For instance, per mayoral request, the funding agency in New York City used its MI system to generate reports of aggregate enrollment by grade level on a monthly basis and by demographic status on a yearly basis and sent them to the mayor's office. In Washington, D.C., a driver for revamping the MI system was the requirement to present data to the mayor at monthly meetings of youth-serving agencies. In contrast, cities with low mayoral demand for data did not tend to prioritize the analysis and use of such data. For instance, Louisville had an incredibly rich data set with links to school-day information; however, data analysis occurred primarily in the district research office, and agency staff reported lacking resources to use the data as much as they wanted.

Multiagency participation in the implementation of the MI system facilitated data sharing and enhanced collaboration. Collaboration increased the likelihood that a school district, for example, would share relevant school data with youth-service agencies to create more targeted services that could improve school-related outcomes (e.g., Louisville). In Chicago, the participation of a large number of agencies helped ensured that consistent information was collected across the multiple agencies overseeing children- and youth-related services.

Formal evaluation helped to ensure analysis and use of data. External evaluations provided cities with analyses that merged multiple sources of data, including the OST MI system, and examined relationships between implementation and outcomes. In these cities, such analyses informed decisions about funding and program development. Positive findings from evaluations helped generate public support or additional funding for OST programs.

Future Steps

One respondent described MI system implementation as an "evolutionary" process. As such, all the cities described future plans that included expanding the abilities of the MI system, its links to other sources of data, and future analyses. New York City officials reported plans to link the MI system with the agency's fiscal department to fully implement a performance-based payment mechanism. San Francisco discussed working toward a centralized MI system that would be shared by multiple city agencies. Washington, D.C., and Louisville described plans to develop a OneCard system that students could use to scan in and out of OST programs, ride public transportation, and check out library books. Louisville respondents also envisioned mapping drop-out rates across the city-county, locations of low-achieving students, and locations of high rates of unemployment to better target program funding to those areas. In Chicago, city leaders wanted to identify geographic areas of the city that were underserved (or overserved) and to compare attendance and demand for services among funding agencies in an effort to drive collaboration, joint planning of services, and adoption of best practices. In Boston, respondents described wanting to link MI system data to the city OST program locator to provide real-time data on the number of slots filled and average attendance per day.

Summary

We found that context drove many of the decisions made in the development of each city's OST MI system. Cities had a variety of goals and constraints when entering into this process, which had implications for the proportion of city-funded providers using the system as well as the presence or absence of data linkages with other information systems in the city. In some cities, the MI system tracked a significant percentage of city-funded OST programs, whereas in other sites, there was more modest design and the MI system captured a smaller share of OST participation. City desire for control over the implementation process led to differing decisions regarding whether to develop the MI system in-house or contract with a vendor of such systems.

MI systems evolved over time—cities added on capabilities, altered which types of data were gathered, and worked to improve their systems to make them more user-friendly. In two cities, changes in city context led to a change of MI system.

City agencies and intermediaries reported seven distinct uses of MI system data. All used the MI systems to gather information on programs and participants (e.g., enrollment, attendance, demographics). The importance of this use alone cannot be underestimated. Prior to MI system adoption, the cities could say little about the programs they funded or the youth being served. Some city agencies focused on a limited set of objectives, such as grant management, while others were at various stages of developing analytical uses for their MI system data to improve the quality and accessibility of OST programming and to examine its effect on student outcomes. New York City stood out in the use of MI system data by the funding agency to direct resources to successful providers and programs. At the time of our study, cities had significant plans for the MI system that included expanding the abilities of the MI system, its links to other sources of data, and future analyses.

We identified a number of factors that influenced the use of MI system data by city agencies and intermediaries, including availability of resources, mayoral demand for data, the collaboration of agencies during development of the MI system, and formal evaluations.

CHAPTER THREE

Ensuring Data Quality

The old maxim, "garbage in, garbage out," applies just as well to the world of OST management information systems as to almost any other sector or business with a need for useful information. As described in the introduction, the accuracy and timeliness of data housed in MI systems is crucial to the value of the system, and inaccurate or late data entry directly affect how system data can be used to inform decisions about OST program policy, planning, and quality improvement. Drawing on interview and survey data, this chapter describes four factors that city officials reported helped improve the quality of data entered into the system: the method of data entry, the immediate use of data by providers, training, and monitoring providers' use of the MI system.

Method of Data Entry

OST providers entered a good deal of participant data into the MI systems. At a minimum, they entered enrollment and attendance data for each participant. When enrolling students in a program, providers input data such as name, age or birth date, parents' names, contact information, emergency contact information, and demographics. Accuracy of this information was important for cities so that they could obtain accurate counts of individual students enrolled in programs. Respondents cited accurate emergency contact information as critical in coordinating a safe system in which schools, provider networks, and families can work together to communicate about the whereabouts of students on a daily basis. Further, for cities that planned to eventually link MI system data with other city data sources, such as school system data, considering methods of ensuring the comparability of data from these systems up front enabled such linkages. As children and youth participate in programming, OST staff must record attendance data in the system and sometimes track student participation in particular activities in the program. In this section, we describe how city respondents thought the method of data entry for enrollment and attendance helped ensure data quality.

Enrollment Data

In three cities, Louisville, Denver, and Providence, OST MI system participant information was populated using school district data. In Louisville, providers entered the name and birth date of a student into the MI system upon enrollment. The MI system linked to a data bridge that populated the MI system with the student's identification number and basic information (name, gender) from the district database. In Denver and Providence, this process was not automatic. Instead, school district data was downloaded into the MI system, typically during the OST enrollment period. These links with school district data served two functions in terms of data quality. First, they improved the accuracy of OST enrollment data by reducing opportunities for data-entry error (e.g., misspelled names, multiple entries for the same participant). However, providers in a few cities considered the OST data to be the best source of contact information because some families moved frequently over the course of the year and often did not update the school. Second, the direct data link eased investigation of relationships between OST attendance and school outcomes. An additional benefit was the time saved because provider staff did not have to request and enter demographic information that already existed in the district data system.

Attendance Data

Each city's MI system was web-based, and this particular quality was cited as an enabler of timely entry of attendance data. In interviews, many providers described older participant-tracking systems that existed on only one computer at the organization. Often, this fixed computing resource was unavailable because it was being used by other school or OST provider staff, so data entry would be delayed or not done at all. Other providers kept attendance records solely on paper and sent them to funders after program sessions were completed. In Chicago, city agency personnel described having files of paper attendance records submitted by OST providers A web-based computerized tracking system removed impediments to timely data submission, as provider staff could access the system from any computer with an Internet connection.

Across the cities, attendance data were entered into MI systems in three ways: (1) youth would scan identification cards upon entry to the program, (2) those directly involved in providing the OST programming or the site coordinator collected and entered the data into the system, or (3) attendance information was collected and passed along to a data manager or administrative assistant to enter. Sources believed that each of these methods provided some advantages over others to ensure the accuracy and timeliness of data entry; however, disadvantages for each were found as well, leaving it unclear whether a universal preferred method of data entry exists.

Having participants scan their own identification cards was touted by some city officials as a highly reliable method of collecting attendance data. With these systems, attendance data were automatically entered into the MI system, and data-entry error was prevented. However, we found the scan technology underused by providers. Provider survey results showed that only 24 percent of providers with scanners in Louisville had students scan their own cards upon arrival to the program. The others still took attendance through a sign-in sheet and either manually entered the data or provider staff would scan participants' cards based on the attendance sheets. In interviews, providers expressed a number of concerns about the scan cards. Some feared that youth participants would lose their cards, which would result in either the provider or the participant having to bear the cost of replacement. Even a $1 replacement fee seemed prohibitive for the low-income participants. The other concern mentioned was that it seemed too impersonal. Finally, providers that tracked youth in different activities preferred attendance rosters because they could not afford to have scanners outside each activity room.

Having those directly involved in providing the OST programming or the site coordinator enter the data (model 2) was also thought to yield highly accurate information, because these staff members had first-hand knowledge of program participants and the program structure. As one interviewee noted, "We learned that by not having knowledge of a program, the data manager would have a harder time than a program coordinator in collecting quality data." For instance, a data manager would not know if a student's attendance was accidently transposed onto another students' record or if a planned activity had been canceled, but a person involved in providing the services would be able to catch those types of errors. However, due to demands on their time, those directly involved in coordinating or providing programs were sometimes forced to put off entering attendance data into the MI system, thus affecting the timeliness of data entry.

The third model was one that generally only larger OST providers could follow: Program management staff handed off data entry to an administrative staff member or data manager. This model removed the burden from program managers and sometimes helped to ensure the timeliness of data entry. However, as mentioned earlier, some thought that administrative staff were more prone to enter erroneous data than were program staff.

Immediate Uses for Data

Across the cities, agency and intermediary leadership thought that MI system data quality improved when provider staff saw its utility and possessed a sense of ownership over the data. As one agency official in Chicago commented,

> Each program needs to use the data to help themselves (sic) first. That will drive good data in the system and increase participation in [the MI system] by providers.

Interviewees in Providence said that daily on-site use of the MI system was a factor that contributed to data accuracy. Providence used MI system data daily to generate transportation routes, so the immediate need for the data motivated timely and accurate input.

Providing Training

Recognizing the need for MI system training for providers, agencies or intermediaries in all cities invested in it. One source described a "learning curve" for many providers who had never before entered data online. Larger cities provided quarterly or monthly training sessions for providers due to the high turnover rate among staff in the OST field. For instance, in New York City, the main funding agency contracted with an external professional development provider to provide monthly training on the MI system. In smaller cities, such as Providence, training was offered to new staff on an as-needed basis after the initial rollout. In Louisville, where providers had access to a separate school district system in addition to the MI system, the district offered training and support on its system as well. In Chicago, consultants were hired to conduct formal training sessions with users and to develop a training manual for each of the four city organizations.

The topics most frequently covered in MI system training were data entry, data retrieval, and how to generate basic reports to track attendance, discontinuance, and absence. These are the basics needed to operate an MI system. Most respondents to the provider survey reported that the training they received was very useful or extremely useful. This was true of two-thirds or more of providers in Chicago, Denver, Louisville, and New York City; about half in Providence and San Francisco; and about two-fifths in Washington, D.C.

In addition to the basic training provided, New York City and San Francisco created intermediate and advanced training sessions for OST agency executive directors and program managers (individuals in charge of an OST program or group of programs). Topics in these courses covered data analysis and interpretation and the creation of summary reports. The text box describes the training provided in San Francisco.

There appears to be substantial demand for additional MI system training. As seen in Table 3.1, at least half of the OST providers in each city reported wanting more training in at least one facet of the system. Some wanted more training in the basic aspects of operating the MI system, such as data entry and retrieval. Even more providers wanted advanced training in how to analyze, interpret, and share information: This was cited by 60 percent or more of OST managers in every city except Washington, D.C.

San Francisco: Evolving Training

In San Francisco, DCYF offered beginner and intermediate training on its MI system, the Contract Management System, once a month to facilitate commitment to using the system and to provide ongoing support. Such frequent training was considered necessary because of high staff turnover. Beginner training sessions focused on the basics of entering data, such as creating participant records, setting up group and individual activities, enrolling participants in group activities, and recording attendance for group activities and contacts for individual services. Intermediate training sessions focused on generating reports and conducting data queries (for example, to compare the attendance of middle school students to that of elementary students). Intermediate training sessions also helped providers understand how the data being entered into the system affected their programs' metrics. For after-school providers, it was especially important to understand how average daily attendance and hours of services were calculated and how mistakes in entering data would lead to inaccurate numbers for the program. For example, if a program did not maintain accurate enrollment data for its group activities, its average hours of service per participant would appear artificially low. Or, if they did not delete a scheduled date for an activity that was canceled, average daily attendance rates would be negatively affected. The beginning and intermediate training was conducted back to back, for two hours each, during the first Tuesday of every month. Training was voluntary, although program officers could mandate that providers attend if their data were problematic or if there had been staff turnover. Training sessions were typically attended by no more than 17 people at a time.

Table 3.1
Percentage of Respondents to Provider Survey Reporting a Desire for Additional Training in Specific Areas

Topic	Chicago (n = 151)	Denver (n = 13)	Louisville (n = 25)	New York City (n = 553)	Providence (n = 18)	San Francisco (n = 124)	Washington, D.C. (n = 18)
Data entry	42	70	47	35	53	29	21
Data retrieval	53	80	90	48	64	56	43
Using the city MI system to track attendance, discontinuance, absence, and other basic information	44	80	63	46	60	43	29
Data analysis and interpretation	67	100	89	67	87	75	57
Creating summary reports	66	91	100	69	73	67	43

NOTE: Response options were "none," "a little," or "a lot." Values reflect the percentage responding "a little" or "a lot."

In addition to the training offered by agencies or intermediaries, MI system vendors also offered an array of supports to users, including 1-800 numbers, online help, lists of frequently asked questions, webinars, and on-site support. In Louisville, a vendor representative visited the city and providers quarterly to offer on-site assistance. In Denver, the vendor provided special on-site training in response to requests from OST providers.

Monitoring Providers' Data Entry

City agencies and intermediaries reported using the MI system to help monitor data timeliness and accuracy. In New York City and San Francisco, the MI system locked out providers who had not entered their attendance data within 14 days. These providers were unable to input information until they spoke to their city program manager to rectify the situation. Similarly, Louisville's MI system flagged providers that did not enter data on a regular basis, allowing the vendor to follow up with that provider and investigate the problem. In addition, each MI system featured data-checking mechanisms to help identify inaccuracies. For instance, officials reported running reports from the MI system to check for duplicate student-level attendance or enrollment data indicating that a participant was in two places at once, a sure sign of inaccurate data. Agency staff in New York City reported comparing hours of participation with the number of available programming hours; a data problem was apparent if the former was larger than the latter.

In New York City, agency staff conducted annual site visits to each program they oversaw to conduct quality assessments. During the visits, agency staff conducted a head count of participants and checked that number against the attendance figures entered into the MI system by the provider. Any large discrepancies were addressed with the provider. In Washington, D.C., the intermediary found a few sites with consistent 100-percent attendance, raising concerns about the validity of those data.

Summary

For the MI system to generate useful data that can inform decisions, data entered into the system must be accurate. Interviewees identified a number of factors that helped ensure the quality of data entered into the MI system. First, a web-based format was considered important because it made the MI system readily accessible and encouraged timely data entry. In Louisville, Denver, and Providence, linking the MI system to district data helped increase the accuracy of student enrollment data. In Providence, where providers used MI system data to manage transportation, interviewees said that the daily need for up-to-date participant information led to greater accuracy and ensured timely data entry. Leaders in some cities thought that data accuracy could be improved by adopting certain methods of data entry (e.g., scan cards) or having certain personnel entering the data, although disadvantages to these methods were also noted. All city agencies and intermediaries invested in training, another key to ensuring accurate, timely data. New York City and San Francisco offered intermediate and advanced training to support data analysis and use, and survey data indicated that this type of training was desired by many providers in other cities as well. Finally, some city agencies and intermediaries also made use of MI system features to help them monitor the timeliness and accuracy of data entered by providers.

CHAPTER FOUR

Providers' Use of Data from Management Information Systems

Providers play a key role in determining the extent to which the adoption of MI systems can bring about improvements in OST provision. Provider organizations are responsible for entering data into the systems. Further, leaders of these organizations can use data from the MI system to inform their own programmatic choices and continuous improvement cycles. In this chapter, we draw on interview and survey data (survey respondents tended to be executive directors or program managers) to describe providers' use of their cities' MI systems, use of data from MI systems, and factors that enabled or constrained providers' use of data. We used statistical modeling to explore relationships between possible enabling and constraining factors and the extent to which providers found their cities' MI system to be useful for their own purposes.

Provider Perceptions About City Management Information Systems

Because provider buy-in was likely to influence the quality of data entered into a city's MI system, we asked providers a series of questions specifically aimed at gauging their level of buy-in and the extent to which they found the city MI system to be useful (see Table 4.1). Overall, we found that the level of provider opinions about cities' OST MI systems was quite positive in each city except Washington, D.C., which is singled out for discussion later.

Table 4.1
Percentage of Providers Agreeing or Strongly Agreeing with Statements About Their City's OST Management Information System

Statement	Chicago (n = 151)	Denver (n = 13)	Louisville (n = 25)	New York City (n = 553)	Providence (n = 18)	San Francisco (n = 124)	Washington, D.C. (n = 18)
The city MI system provides me with valuable information about my OST programs	84	100	95	91	93	86	40
If my organization was not required to use the city MI system, we would not use it anymore	37	8	26	36	27	39	73
I share reports generated from the city MI system with my program staff	74	100	85	74	80	69	13
My staff does not fully understand why we enter data into the city MI system	26	50	35	18	40	24	27
The city MI system has improved communication between our program and our funders	68	100	65	76	67	76	20

NOTE: The total number of respondents (n) is included for reference. Response options were "strongly disagree," "disagree," "agree," or "strongly agree."

Across the other cities, 84–100 percent of providers agreed that the city MI system provided valuable information about their OST programs. As one San Francisco provider explained in response to an open-ended survey question,

> Although data entry can put a strain on the agency due to time restrictions (not enough time for staff to enter data), the programs greatly benefit from the information derived from the [MI system]. The information helps in many ways such as program management, program evaluation, program planning and fund development, and quality assurance.

In fact, few providers agreed that entering data into the MI system was a waste of staff time (0–20 percent, depending on the city).

Providers reported sharing MI system–generated reports with program staff (69–100 percent of providers in each city) and agreed that the system had improved communication between the program and funders (65–100 percent). In interviews, providers in Denver and Chicago noted that the MI system had made it easier to generate reports and had improved communication with funders. Providers in Chicago further indicated that the MI system was useful in preparing program descriptions and attendance reports for use in RFP responses.

On the survey, one provider in Louisville described how the ability to provide hard data on programming aided fundraising efforts:

> Although data entry is a definite strain on my staff, it proved to be very worth it. Recently, due to the economic hard times, one of our funders that represents 50 percent of the funding for my staff positions was considering cutting funding for our programs. Thanks to the information from [the MI system], we were able to show how many students we were serving and it made such an impact that our funding is intact.

In considering the somewhat positive views expressed and the benefits reported by providers, it is important to note that the majority of respondents had been using the MI system for a number of years. In interviews, city officials noted that there was more resistance among providers during initial system implementation. For instance, respondents in Louisville said that providers were initially reluctant to implement the MI system because they viewed it as a monitoring tool rather than a way to help them improve the delivery of services. City funders took the approach of trying to gain more buy-in by explaining that they intended to help providers achieve desired results through a more systematic approach to gathering and reporting attendance and linking it to outcome data. Furthermore, they argued, it would help providers showcase their accomplishments and potentially gain access to more resources. Similarly, a prior study found that providers embraced MI systems over time, after they realized that reports enhanced staff's ability to communicate with parents, assess the participation patterns of students, assist in organizational planning for the changing demographics of the population served (e.g., students getting older), and maintain increased internal accountability (Herrera and Arbreton, 2003).

In the majority of cases, resistance to the MI systems appeared to have dissipated, and some providers expressed a desire for their cities' MI systems to have more expansive capabilities. As one provider in San Francisco noted,

> I would love to see more organizational support capabilities with our [MI system]—being able to create surveys, staff development, training, evaluation, progress tracking, parent communications, [for example].

These positive views were contrasted by those expressed by providers in Washington, D.C., where only 40 percent of providers agreed that the city MI system provided valuable information, 13 percent reported sharing reports with staff, and 20 percent reported that the MI system improved communication with funders. A few factors may have influenced these differences in perception among providers in Washington, D.C. First, the majority of providers there used at least one other MI system. Second, sources in Washington, D.C., perceived the city's MI system as oriented toward contract management and compliance. According to one provider:

> [The city MI system] may provide data for funders but hasn't really been developed to be a planning and evaluation tool designed to provide relevant help for our mission, . . . or at least it's never been posed in those terms. Really just described as a way to track attendance and budgets.

As discussed in Chapter Two, in spring 2009, an intermediary in Washington, D.C., adopted a new MI system to support a wider range of goals and provide additional tools for providers to manage their programs.

Providers, regardless of city, found the MI system less useful if they considered it an external monitoring tool rather than an internal management tool. One provider in Providence expressed this sentiment plainly: "This system was not designed to help me. It is used by someone else to monitor me. Therefore its usefulness to me is lost."

How Providers Use Management Information System Data

Because we were interested in how the use of data can support improvements in OST programming, we were interested in how providers used MI system data broadly—from any MI system, not just their cities' systems. Providers reported making multiple uses of data from these various MI systems. More than 70 percent of providers in each city reported using MI system data for day-to-day program management, program monitoring, and participant tracking (see Table 4.2). According to one provider,

> [The MI system] has been a great tool for our organization. It can give us a snapshot of attendance, daily activities, etc. It helps us monitor increase/decrease in attendance. It makes our youth responsible by having them sign in each day. Our youth look forward to signing in.

At least half of the providers across the cities reported using data in more sophisticated ways, such as to inform program improvement

Table 4.2
Percentage of Respondents Using Data from Any Management Information System for Various Activities

Activity	Chicago (n = 151)	Denver (n = 13)	Louisville (n = 25)	New York City (n = 553)	Providence (n = 18)	San Francisco (n = 124)	Washington, D.C. (n = 18)
Day-to-day program management (e.g., printing out attendance sheets)	86	73	80	74	100	75	73
Participation tracking	84	91	86	80	79	85	93
Program monitoring	81	91	76	75	86	75	93
Program improvement	74	89	67	72	57	61	87
Developing new programs	60	75	62	57	50	49	60
Case management	38	37	33	29	23	30	47
Reporting to funders	67	67	86	56	57	84	86
Marketing materials for parents and youth	29	11	33	31	29	29	47
Developing proposals	62	50	67	45	31	62	60
Identifying staffing needs	35	60	52	37	29	36	53
Sharing reports and findings with other youth-supporting organizations	29	75	52	34	43	40	47

NOTE: The total number of respondents (n) is included for reference.

and program development. In most cities, at least one in four providers used data from an MI system for case management, marketing activities, developing proposals, identifying staffing needs, and sharing reports with other youth-supporting organizations. Further, across the cities, 53–100 percent of providers reported that MI system data improved their ability to set goals and monitor the progress of their programs. On the open-ended survey response, providers described this benefit:

> It is very helpful in tracking daily attendance and student participation in our site and in other sites across the city. It is a valuable tool to help us access how we are doing and how it compares to student participation in the past. It is also helpful to track student interest in specific programs to know if and when they should be offered.

> Management information systems have been extremely important in building the capacity of our organization and sustainability. To be able to regularly collect and analyze data [related] to programming attendance, participant make up, programming outcomes, and staff and volunteer contributions has not only helped our organization to continue to improve upon our efforts, but has made what we do clear and transparent to employees, our board of directors, other youth agencies, and funders, ultimately resulting in better program offerings to youth. . . . Management information systems have provided our agency a tool to regularly evaluate ourselves and share our successes, as well as needs for improvement, with the community.

Factors That Enabled or Constrained Providers' Use of Data

As described in Chapter One, prior research posits that a number of factors may enable or constrain the use of data from an MI system, including ease of use, resources available to providers, and the capacity of providers to use technological tools.

User-Friendly Systems

In all cities, MI systems were typically considered user-friendly. Across cities, 73–91 percent of OST providers agreed or strongly agreed that the MI system was easy to use and understand (see Table 4.3). Approximately 40 percent or fewer providers agreed or strongly agreed that the MI system was difficult to navigate, had too many screens to navigate, or sometimes crashed and lost information.

Staffing and Resources

Providers reported facing a variety of challenges when using the MI system and its data, some of which were related to staffing and resource constraints. Frequent staff turnover was reported as a challenge by at least 25 percent of managers in every city (see Table 4.4). Many providers also reported a lack of computer skills among staff and a lack of IT support. Moreover, between 37 and 73 percent of managers agreed that a lack of resources (e.g., time, personnel) prevented them from fully utilizing the system(s). As one provider from Denver noted,

> When all the advantages of [the MI system] can be accessed, the rewards are great. Having the time to utilize all the reports and information that can be acquired is challenging.

Particularly for smaller providers, data-entry requirements can strain capacity so much that there is little left to make use of the data. Indeed, about a quarter or more OST providers reported that data-entry requirements strained their organizations' capacity and that it was difficult to keep up with all the reporting requirements. One provider from Chicago described how capacity issues constrained the use of the MI system data, even when there was buy-in for its use:

> In my opinion, the whole concept of management information systems is fundamentally sound and will eventually become extremely useful. However, for small organizations like ours, unless funding and personnel problems are solved, it will be challenging to get the most out of the system. For now it is a tool we see as being very useful up the road. We see potential and hope to be able to take advantage of it in the near future.

Table 4.3
Percentage of Providers Agreeing or Strongly Agreeing with Statements About Usability of City OST Management Information Systems

Statement	Chicago (n = 151)	Denver (n = 13)	Louisville (n = 25)	New York City (n = 553)	Providence (n = 18)	San Francisco (n = 124)	Washington, D.C. (n = 18)
The city MI system is easy to use and to understand	84	91	81	83	80	86	73
The city MI system permits me to enter data over multiple sessions without losing the place where I left off	82	100	62	66	100	92	73
I encounter problems when trying to navigate through the screens	30	18	24	25	40	26	27
There are too many screens that I need to navigate through to enter my specific data	34	18	29	31	33	35	33
I often have to enter the same data into the city MI system over and over again	33	9	5	34	53	33	33
The city MI system tends to crash and sometimes loses information that I need	15	18	11	27	13	16	13

NOTE: The total number of respondents (n) is included for reference. Response options were "strongly disagree," "disagree," "agree," or "strongly agree."

Table 4.4
Percentage of Providers Agreeing or Strongly Agreeing with Statements About Resource Constraints Inhibiting Data Use and Entry

Statement	Chicago (n = 151)	Denver (n = 13)	Louisville (n = 25)	New York City (n = 553)	Providence (n = 18)	San Francisco (n = 124)	Washington, D.C. (n = 18)
Data entry requirements strain the capacity of my organization	41	27	40	23	40	38	33
Network problems make it difficult for my staff to enter data	25	18	25	29	27	30	13
It is difficult for me and my staff to keep up with all our reporting requirements	38	36	42	25	60	37	33
Frequent staff turnover is a challenge for my organization	28	50	45	31	47	25	27
Lack of IT support hinders my or my staff's ability to address problems with the system(s) when they come up	31	20	42	26	36	36	7
Lack of resources (e.g., time, personnel) prevents us from fully utilizing the system(s)	59	55	68	37	73	65	50

NOTE: The total number of respondents (n) is included for reference. Response options were "strongly disagree," "disagree," "agree," or "strongly agree."

Indeed, imposing greater requirements on providers to use MI systems could crowd out very small "mom-and-pop" providers in favor of larger providers with greater capacity. This study did not gather evidence of whether this had occurred. However, anecdotally, a few study participants in cities that had been using their MI systems for a longer period thought that this may have occurred to some extent. If such crowding out were to occur, it is not known whether it would affect the quality or range of OST opportunities for children or youth.

City officials also expressed concerns about provider capacity to use the MI system and skills to make good use of the data. As one respondent stated,

> There's the data system but there's also the comfort with data and the use of data. I think that is also a challenge, and I think a lot of people don't integrate data into their thinking. It's going in, but once they get it out, they don't know what to do with it.

Multiple Management Information Systems

In light of the growing availability of MI systems in the OST field, many funders require that OST programs use them. Some provider organizations also use such systems to track programming for internal purposes. Consequently, for many providers in our study, the city-required MI system was not the only one they used. In some cities, the use of multiple MI systems was more prevalent than in others. The use of more than one MI system ranged from 14 percent of providers in Providence to 67 percent of providers in Washington, D.C (see Table 4.5). In fact, in Washington, D.C., 54 percent of providers reported being required to use three or more MI systems.

The need to enter data into multiple MI systems or the ability to enter only partial data into an MI system posed challenges for providers. Some providers were frustrated that the city MI system would not accept uploads of data already entered into other systems, creating additional data-entry work for providers. One Chicago survey respondent explained the difficulties and frustration of using multiple MI systems:

Table 4.5
Percentage of Providers in Each City, by Number of Management Information Systems in Use

Number of MI Systems	Chicago (n = 151)	Denver (n = 13)	Louisville (n = 25)	New York City (n = 553)	Providence (n = 18)	San Francisco (n = 124)	Washington, D.C. (n = 18)
1	55	73	52	66	87	57	33
2	23	9	19	16	7	22	13
3	13	9	29	10	7	14	27
4 or more	10	9	0	8	0	7	27

NOTE: The total number of respondents (n) is included for reference.

We all understand the need for a MI system. However, when an organization is funded by federal, state, and city contracts and each . . . requires a MI system, our staff have to enter the same client information . . . into five different databases. Government agencies need to collaborate better and have a coordinated MI system effort. It is a waste of staff time to enter the same information into so many databases—and this is an activity that no government grant is willing to pay for.

It is also important to note that the various agency MI systems in Chicago were separate systems, and providers funded through multiple city agencies were required to enter data into each separate system. A couple of providers expressed the desire for these city MI systems to interface with one another.

The city agencies in New York City and San Francisco and the intermediary in Providence tried to address the duplication issue to some extent by building in mechanisms for consolidating data entry. In New York City, the agency added new fields and modified existing ones so that providers could enter data on children in programs receiving funding from other sources and still be in compliance with reporting requirements. In Providence, the MI system was built to help complete annual reports for 21st Century Community Learning Center funding, and providers reported efficiencies in fulfilling both reporting requirements. In San Francisco, the city agency supported ten large programs by permitting them to import data from another MI system into the city MI system.

Providers using their own internal MI systems to monitor programming, staffing, and quality tended to be particularly frustrated with city MI system mandates. As one Washington, D.C., survey respondent wrote,

> MI systems are critical elements to a well run organization. We had devoted a great deal of time, energy and resources to create the most efficient and user friendly system for our specific programming. Donor advised or required MI systems were less efficient, less user friendly, and less reliable. It created a situation where double entry was required—and that was difficult to manage.

Examining the Relationship Between Constraints and Perceived Usefulness of City MI Systems

We used a regression model to explore the relationship between enablers and constraints and the extent to which providers perceived the city's OST MI system to be useful for their own purposes.[1] The dependent variable was a scale of five survey items that measured the usefulness of the MI system from the provider perspective. As independent variables we included measures of the perceived quality of MI system training, how user-friendly the MI system was, OST staff and resource constraints, whether it was the provider's first year using the MI system, and whether the provider used additional MI systems (see the appendix for variable definitions and the reliability of the survey scales).

The results were as follows, controlling for other variables in the model (see Table 4.6):

---

[1] To control for differences across cities and differing sample sizes across cities, we included a set of indicator variables for the cities in the study. These controls were important because the contextual factors varied so much from city to city.

Table 4.6
Results from Model Estimating the Relationship Between Various Enablers or Challenges and the Perceived Usefulness of City Management Information Systems

Enabler or Challenge and Site	Regression Coefficient
High-quality training	0.235*** (0.058)
User-friendly	0.340*** (0.059)
Staff and resource constraints	−0.080 (0.055)
More than one MI system	−0.129* (0.060)
Personally used system for one year or more	0.147** (0.057)
Chicago	0.023 (0.072)
Denver	0.140 (0.131)
Louisville	0.057 (0.082)
Providence	0.038 (0.103)
San Francisco	−0.042 (0.065)
Washington, D.C.	−0.568*** (0.124)

NOTE: The dependent variable is a scale measuring the usefulness of the city MI system. See the appendix for details. This variable has a mean of 2.9 and a standard deviation of 0.5. * = significant at the 0.05 level; ** = significant at the 0.01 level; *** = significant at the 0.001 level. Variable values are not standardized. Standard errors are given in parentheses. New York City is the excluded reference category.

- Providers' rating of the quality of MI system training had a positive and significant association with the perceived usefulness of the city MI system, suggesting a payoff for high-quality training.

- The extent to which the MI system was considered user-friendly was positively and significantly associated with the perceived usefulness of the city MI system. This finding suggests the need for data systems that are user-friendly and designed to minimize problems and frustration.
- Ratings of the usefulness of the MI system were significantly higher among providers that had been using the system for one year or longer. This suggests that there is a learning curve associated with a new MI system and that providers become more positive about the systems after the first year.
- Providers that reported using more than one MI system had significantly lower perceptions of city MI system usefulness.
- Even controlling for other factors, providers in Washington, D.C., had significantly lower perceptions of that city's MI system usefulness compared to other cities. This finding suggests that contextual factors in Washington, D.C., lowered perceptions of the usefulness of data from the MI system.
- Our measure of staff and resource constraints was negatively associated with perceptions of MI system usefulness, but the association was not statistically significant when controlling for other factors.

Summary

Prior research shows that, for MI systems to support OST improvement at the provider and city levels, providers must support the MI system, enter accurate data, and use the data to improve their programs. In fact, we found that the majority of providers did buy into their cities' OST MI systems and used the data for such purposes as program management, program improvement, and providing information to funders. In addition, they typically found their cities' MI systems to be user-friendly. Many providers reported having to use more than one MI system—either for other funders or to support their own organization's improvement needs. For many providers, this requirement created strain on staff and necessitated duplicate data entry. Our modeling results showed that using multiple MI systems was negatively related to the perceived usefulness of the city MI system. A substantial minority of providers reported constraints on MI system use, such as staff turnover, staff computer skills, IT support, and a lack of resources (e.g., time, personnel). In our modeling, though, these constraints were not significantly related to how useful the providers found the city MI system. A number of factors were positively and significantly related to our perceived usefulness scale in the model, including high-quality training, the extent to which the system was considered user-friendly, and having used the MI system for more than one year.

CHAPTER FIVE

Conclusion

This monograph focused on one mechanism that can be used to facilitate the flow of information among key stakeholders in an OST system to improve decisionmaking—the adoption of web-based MI systems. MI systems can help improve OST provision by providing city agencies, intermediaries, and providers with valuable and comparable information about programming and participation. Theoretically, if stakeholders used the data generated by these systems in decisionmaking, it could lead to improved OST services and access to programming for children and youth, which could, in turn, lead to better outcomes for participants. At the city level, current information on enrollment and participation gives city managers rough indicators of a program's interest to students (enrollment) and quality (participation). City managers can use this information to identify potentially struggling programs and intercede with support, determine which programs or types of programs to fund based on historical enrollment figures, and place programs in specific areas of the city with higher demand. Furthermore, providers can use their own data to modify programs midcourse, follow up with students to encourage participation, and plan future programs more effectively.

The eight cities in this study increase our understanding of how a city MI system can be used at the city and provider levels, as well as the challenges stakeholders face in developing and using such systems and their data. In this chapter, we present a summary and discussion of key findings and lessons for the field that emerged from these findings.

Summary of Key Findings

The OST field is relatively new to developing MI systems and using their data to inform decisions. At the beginning of this monograph, we posited that, for an MI system to be used to support improvements in an OST system, (1) providers must enter timely and accurate information into the MI system, (2) stakeholders (city agencies, intermediaries, and providers) must analyze (or hire an evaluator to analyze) the data and then report them to decisionmakers, and (3) decisionmakers must act on the data. Indeed, we found evidence that, overall, condition 1 had been met and that there was real progress in most cities on conditions 2 and 3. In most cities, data actions (by agency funders and providers) focused on supporting individual program improvement. However, in some cities, data were used to consider resource allocation to programs and target populations. At the time of the last round of data collection in the spring of 2009, the case-study cities did not consider their work in this area to be complete and had future plans, but all had made substantial progress. We found that city officials and OST providers shared the vision that MI systems can gather information to support system and program improvement. Our specific findings are reviewed here.

City context drove development decisions. Each city had a unique context and goals that shaped some overarching development decisions. The cities all had unique initial goals (e.g., improving contract management, coordinating in-school and after-school data) and constraints (e.g., lack of funding) that led varying proportions of OST providers to use the MI system and the presence or absence of data linkages with other information systems in the city. Chicago stood out in the use of best practices in terms of carefully mapping organizational goals for data collection during the development phase. Varying desire for control over the data led to differing decisions regarding whether to develop the MI system in-house or contract with an external vendor. We found no concrete evidence to suggest that in-house development or outsourcing to an external vendor was preferable.

MI systems evolved over time. Many of the cities made modifications to enhance their MI systems over time. Cities developed new capabilities for their systems, such as the ability to process RFPs; changed the type of data gathered; and worked to make the systems more user-friendly. Changing context in two cities (Boston and Washington, D.C.) led to the adoption of new MI systems to meet new or growing needs. One respondent described MI system implementation as an "evolutionary" process. As such, cities' future plans included expanding the abilities of their MI systems and linking them to other sources of data. For instance, New York City officials reported plans to link the MI system with the agency's fiscal department to fully implement a performance-based payment mechanism, and San Francisco respondents discussed working toward a centralized MI system that would be shared by multiple city agencies.

MI systems gave cities much-needed data about OST programming and participation, which they used to improve programs. All the cities used data from their MI systems to better understand OST programming and participation (e.g., enrollment, attendance, demographics). The importance of this use cannot be underestimated. Prior to MI system adoption, the cities could say little about the programs they funded or the youth being served. City officials put this information to work to improve participation and programming. For instance, funding partners in Denver used MI system data to identify population groups prone to dropping out of OST programs and found that middle school students were particularly likely to drop out of programming. Subsequently, the partners worked with OST site coordinators to design programs that would better engage this age group. While all cities cited examples of using data to motivate improvement, most wanted to go much further in their analysis and use of the data. For instance, Louisville respondents envisioned mapping dropout rates across the city-county, locations of low-achieving students, and locations of high rates of unemployment to target program funding in those areas. In Chicago, city leaders wanted to identify geographic areas of the city that were underserved (or overserved) and to compare attendance and demand for services among the different funding agencies in an effort to drive collaboration, joint planning of services, and adoption of best practices.

MI system data improved OST contract management and shifted its nature to focus on the quality of programming. Agency and intermediary leaders in Chicago, New York City, San Francisco, and Washington, D.C., all reported that they used their MI system data to improve contract management. In New York City and Chicago, we were told that the collection and use of data shifted the nature of contract management. According to interviewees, prior to implementing their MI systems, cities' management of OST providers was strictly contractual and focused on "paper" rather than programs. With MI system data, they were able to focus on program quality, and city managers used average daily attendance reports to identify potential quality problems and then worked with providers to determine whether they needed assistance.

Cities used MI system data to make funding decisions and to lobby for additional funding. Two cities used MI system data to inform how they funded providers. In Providence, intermediary leaders used past enrollment reports as one source of information during funding review meetings. New York City formally used its MI system as a basis for provider compensation and reduced funding to providers that did not meet attendance targets.

Agencies and intermediaries also reported using MI system data to justify their petitions for continued or additional funding. In Providence, the intermediary presented MI system reports to the PASA board of directors, city council, and funders and used the reports to raise support for city OST efforts. In New York City, the main funding agency reported using MI system information on programming and students served to help generate increased funding from the city, from $46.6 million in FY 2006 to $118.2 million in FY 2009. Respondents described having a competitive advantage over other agencies that were not able to demonstrate program results through data. It seems that the link between the data and successful funding bids will help ensure the continued use of MI systems.

Sharing data from the MI system led to greater coordination among stakeholders. We found a wide range of OST data-sharing agreements across the study sites. Some cities shared MI system reports with other city agencies but did not link the MI system to other data systems. Other cities established agreements to link the MI system to school outcomes to allow an assessment of the relationship between OST participation and children and youth outcomes. Providence, Louisville, and Denver each linked MI system data to school district data and studied the links between OST participation and school outcomes. Louisville stood out in that it gave providers ongoing access to a set of district student-level data; thus, providers could look at the school-day attendance and grades of their participants on an ongoing basis. The small number of providers and the high level of trust among stakeholders in Louisville facilitated this arrangement. This level of provider access to school data would be highly improbable in cities with a very large number of providers (e.g., New York City).

Mayoral demand for data appeared to be a key enabler of city use of data. Resources, particularly time, were limited for city officials. Without a demand for data at the highest levels, some found it difficult to prioritize analyzing data even when they desired to do so. However, mayoral demand for data required city officials to set aside time and prioritize activities and resources in order to analyze, report, and use the MI system data. For instance, in New York City, the funding agency ensured that data were entered into the MI system and developed the capacity to analyze those data to provide regular progress reports to the mayor's office. In Washington, D.C., a number of ongoing initiatives to establish data-sharing mechanisms, revamp the current MI system, and develop analytical capabilities were a direct result of mayoral demand for a renewed commitment to OST system improvement through data use.

All cities invested in efforts to improve data quality. Cities took a variety of approaches to ensuring the quality of entered data. Two cities uploaded participant data from district databases to ensure the accuracy of student enrollment information. Some city officials touted having participants scan their own identification cards as a highly reliable method of collecting attendance data. However, we found the scan technology underused by providers in cities that supported it. Interviewees in Providence said that daily on-site use of the MI system (e.g., generating transportation routes) contributed to data accuracy. City agencies and intermediaries reported using the MI system to help monitor data timeliness and accuracy. For instance, agency staff in New York City reported comparing hours of participation with the number of available programming hours; a data problem was apparent if the former was larger than the latter. All cities provided training to overcome the MI system "learning curve" for providers, many of whom had never entered data online prior to using the system. The majority of providers appreciated the training and wanted more of it, particularly advanced training in data analysis.

Many providers reported using data from the MI system; however, they also reported constraints that limited their use of the data. The majority of providers agreed that their city's MI system provided valuable information about OST programs and reported a number of uses for the data, including program management, program improvement, providing information to funders, and lobbying for additional funding. Some providers expressed a desire to do more with the data, and a few described using MI system data as part of a continuous improvement process. However, even when there was support for the MI system and a desire to use its data, providers identified capacity constraints that limited their ability to make use of the data (e.g., time, personnel, expertise) and frustration if they had to enter data into more than one MI system. In fact, those who reported using more than one MI system had significantly lower perceptions of city MI system usefulness.

Cities' efforts to provide high-quality training paid off, and providers' ratings of the quality of MI system training had a positive and significant association with the perceived usefulness of the city MI system. Finally, providers who had been using the city MI system longer were more likely to view it positively. This suggests that there is a learning curve associated with a new MI system and that perceptions of usefulness improve after the first year.

Lessons for an Emerging Field

While each of the sites experienced the development and implementation of MI systems in different ways, many of the factors that constrained or enabled the systems' use were shared. These experiences point to the following lessons for other cities interested in improving OST provision through the use of data:

- *MI systems are capable of supporting OST system improvement but will not do so without careful planning.* Cities in the study faced a number of decisions during the development phase that affected the ways in which the MI systems could be used. The lesson is that a clear understanding of the goals for the data, including how they support larger OST system-building goals, is a prerequisite for an effective MI system. In addition, it might be necessary to modify the MI system based on experience to enhance its utility. Likewise, cities had to adopt methods of breaking down barriers to the systems' use, such as training, dedication of staff time for data analysis, or the hiring of external evaluators.
- *Using data to showcase OST efforts can lead to additional funding and support.* City leaders and providers reported that the ability to show their funders enrollment, participation, and outcome data led to increases in resources and provided them with a competitive advantage over others seeking funding.
- *Customization of web-based systems encouraged MI system use.* MI system users typically thought the systems were easy to use and said that the web-based interface, implemented in all the cities we examined, encouraged timely data entry because it could be accessed from multiple locations. Moreover, customization of the MI systems to meet the specific needs of city agencies and providers led to greater use of the systems and their data.
- *Investing in high-quality training reaps benefits.* Providers who reported receiving high-quality training were more likely than others to believe that the city MI system was useful. All cities provided training to providers and to city-level program officers to familiarize them with the MI system. Training was also necessary in how to make use of MI system data, including how data analysis can inform improvement efforts. Providers' demand for training was high, and they particularly wanted more advanced training in data analysis and the use of data. In the OST field in

particular, analytical approaches to using data constitute a relatively new and developing field, and most providers may require some level of training and support in the ways in which the system can be used to make improvements to programming.

- *Mechanisms to eliminate redundancies in data entry and reporting requirements would help providers.* One of the most significant constraints to the use of the city MI system was the burden of entering data into multiple systems. This problem manifested not only in the different types of information required by funders, but also in that some providers had to enter the same information into multiple MI systems. If cities hope to increase the accuracy and timely entry of data into MI systems, as well as increase their use, efforts to reduce the burden of repetitive data entry would be helpful. One solution is to engage in better coordination at the city level across agencies and implement a common MI system, which would solve the issue of multiple city-required MI systems. Another option is to configure the city MI system to allow providers to enter data required by other funders. Additional fields were added to New York City's MI system for this purpose. A third option is to allow providers to upload data generated by other MI systems into the city MI system, as was done in some instances in San Francisco.

A Parting Thought

This monograph documented the efforts of eight cities to develop and use data from MI systems to improve OST provision. The OST field is relatively new to developing MI systems and using their data. Many of the cities we studied did not consider their MI system work to be complete, yet they had all made substantial progress. Simply having data on the programs and the youth served is a major, positive step. City officials and OST providers share a vision that MI systems can gather information to support OST system improvement. While cities and providers all face resource constraints that affect analysis and use of data, leaders can foster these activities through incentives. Overall, the adoption of MI systems appears to be a positive step for the field and will likely be a source of continued progress.

.

Survey Administration, Sampling, Weighting, and Modeling

Much of MI system effectiveness hinges on OST programs' use of and commitment to the MI system, so obtaining a full understanding of how OST programs use the system and factors that help or hinder its effective use was key to the study. Due to the large number of providers in many cities, a survey was needed to obtain such information. In this appendix, we describe the sampling procedures, administration, response rates, and development and use of sampling weights for the survey of OST providers.

Sample

From each city, we obtained a list of OST programs that included the name and email address of the program manager and the OST program mailing address. The size of the population of OST programs using each city's MI system varied widely. For instance, Washington, D.C., listed 18 programs, while New York listed 625. Because we wanted to use the survey data to describe activities at each individual site as well as across all surveyed sites, we needed to ensure that a large enough number of providers responded to detect moderate differences at a 0.05 significance level within and across city sites. Based on power calculations,[1] we decided to survey the entire population of programs

---

[1] For the power calculations, we assumed a response rate of 70 percent for most cities and a response rate of at least 80 percent in cities with a small number of programs. We also

in all cities except New York City. For New York City, we estimated that a random sample of 225 programs, about 35 percent, would be sufficient. We stratified this sample to ensure adequate representation among two small groups of programs: those operating on Staten Island and those operating an "option 2" program. Programs in these groups were sampled at twice the rate of other programs.

Table A.1 shows the number of providers by city. Note that, for Washington, D.C., the list includes only providers that were part of the Project My Time initiative, funded by The Wallace Foundation, and not all programs using the Trust's MI system. For Chicago, we were provided with a list of OST programs funded by FSS but not programs funded by CPS or the Chicago Park District, which were also using MI systems. In San Francisco, we focused on and surveyed providers using DCYF's MI system. In Boston, we were unable to conduct a survey because the new MI system was still in development.

In several cases, we were unable to reach the contact provided; in others, the contact person was no longer with the program, but we were able to locate a replacement contact. These cases remained in our sample and are listed in the third column of Table A.1. Other cases, listed in the fourth column, were dropped from our sample as ineligible because they were listed twice or because our attempts to contact the person or program failed. We assumed that, if the city did not have any usable contact information for a program, the program was no longer active.

Administration and Response Rates

We used survey administration procedures that RAND has found to maximize response rates. Respondents had the option to complete the survey either online or on paper. Program officers first received a personalized email invitation to complete the survey online. A few

---

assumed much variability between programs in the same city due to differences in services provided, locales served, and so on, so the expectation was that there would be little clustering among programs within the same city.

Table A.1
Number of Providers Contacted for the Survey, by Site

Site	Providers in City-Supplied List	Providers with Incorrect Contact Information but Located	Duplicates and Providers with Invalid Contact Information That Were Not Located	Total Providers Contacted
Chicago	153	9	14	139
Denver	16	1	2	14
Louisville	25	1	0	25
Providence	24	0	5	19
New York City	625	8	42	183
San Francisco	134	1	8	126
Washington, D.C.	18	0	0	18
Total	995	20	71	524

NOTE: We sampled and attempted to contact 225 providers in New York City.

rounds of personalized email reminders to complete the survey were sent to nonrespondents; we then followed up by sending a hard copy of the survey to those who still had not responded. In our study sites with a small population of programs (and in any sites that were lagging in response), we followed up again with nonrespondents via telephone calls and/or faxes.

We offered incentives to surveyed program officers to boost response rates. We provided a $25 gift certificate to all surveyed program officers, which they could use for themselves or to make a small purchase for their programs. The survey was administered from January through April 2009. As shown in Table A.2, we surveyed a total of 524 programs and received responses from 358, for an overall response rate of 68 percent. City-level response rates varied from 93 percent in Denver to 58 percent in Chicago.

Survey Weights

Sampling probabilities and response rates varied by city and, within New York City, also by strata. To adjust for these differences, we created weights that reflected both the sampling probabilities and response

Table A.2
Survey Response Rates, by Site

Site	Number Contacted	Number Responding	Response Rate (%)
Chicago	139	81	58
Denver	14	13	93
Louisville	25	21	84
Providence	19	15	79
New York City	183	126	69
San Francisco	126	87	69
Washington, D.C.	18	15	83
Total	524	358	68

rates in each city and strata to help ensure that our responding sample would be representative of the population of programs in each of the seven study cities and across all seven cities. (Remember that Boston was excluded from this analysis because its MI system was still under development at the time of our study.) We use these weighted data in our cross-tabulations and models.

Survey Analyses

We conducted site-specific, basic tabulations and developed scales around certain constructs from our survey data (e.g., perceived usefulness of the data). We also ran regression analyses to examine correlations between various predictors and the perceived usefulness of the data. To conduct this simple regression model, we used Proc Survey Reg in SAS, with site-specific dummy variables to control for differences in the size of our sites.

Modeling the Relationship Between Constraints and Perceived Usefulness

To understand the relationship between many of these enablers and constraints and providers' perceptions of city MI system usefulness while controlling for the other factors, we used OLS regression. Table A.3 presents the variables in our model and their definitions. The dependent variable in our model was a scale of five survey items that measures the perceived usefulness of the city MI systems, derived through factor analysis.

We included the following independent variables: measures of the quality of MI system training and the extent to which the MI system was considered user-friendly. We also included a measure of OST staff and resource constraints that the providers' experienced when using the MI system, as well as whether the OST program used any additional MI systems. To control for differences and differing sample sizes across cities, we included a set of indicator variables for the cities in the study. These controls were important because the contextual factors varied so much from city to city.

Table A.3
Definitions of Variables Used in Modeling

Constructs	Definitions
Dependent Variable	
Perceived usefulness of MI system scale (alpha = 0.73)	To what extent do you agree or disagree with the following statements about the city MI system?
	The MI system provides me with valuable information about my OST programs.
	If my organization was not required to use the city MI system, we would not use it anymore.
	I share reports generated from the MI system with my program staff.
	My staff does not fully understand why we enter data in the city MI system.
	The MI system has improved communication between our program and our funders.
	Measured on a 4-point scale (strongly disagree, disagree, agree, strongly agree); statements in italics were reverse-coded
	Mean = 2.86; standard deviation = 0.52
Independent Variables	
Perceived quality of MI system training	How useful was the MI system training you received?
	Defined as 1 if respondent answered extremely useful or very useful on a 4-point scale (extremely useful, very useful, somewhat useful, not useful); otherwise, defined as 0
	Mean = 0.59; standard deviation = 0.49

Table A.3—Continued

Constructs	Definitions
User-friendly MI system scale (alpha = 0.78)	To what extent do you agree or disagree with the following statements about the city MI system?
	The MI system is easy to use and to understand.
	The MI system permits me to enter data over multiple sessions without losing the place where I left off.
	I encounter problems when trying to navigate through the screens.
	There are too many screens that I need to navigate through to enter my specific data.
	I often have to enter the same data in the MI system over and over again.
	The MI system tends to crash and sometimes loses information that I entered.
	Measured on a 4-point scale (strongly disagree, disagree, agree, strongly agree) statements in italics were reverse-coded
	Mean = 2.88; standard deviation = 0.49
Staff/resource constraint scale (alpha = 0.71)	To what extent do you agree or disagree with the following statements about the use of management information system(s)?
	Frequent staff turnover is a challenge for my organization.
	Lack of IT support hinders my or my staff's ability to address problems with the system(s) when they come up.
	Many of my staff lack basic computer skills.
	Lack of resources (e.g., time, personnel) prevents us from fully utilizing the system(s).
	Measured on a 4-point scale (strongly disagree, disagree, agree, strongly agree)
	Mean = 2.20; standard deviation = 0.56

Table A.3—Continued

Constructs	Definitions
Use more than one MI system	How many other MI systems do you or your staff members utilize in your program? Defined as 1 if one or more other systems are reported; otherwise, defined as 0 Mean = 0.40; standard deviation = 0.49
Length of time using MI system	How long have you personally been using the MI system? Defined as 1 if respondent has used the MI system for a year or longer; otherwise, defined as 0 Mean = 0.80; standard deviation = 0.40
City	An indicator variable for each city was defined as 1 if the program was located in that city and 0 if located in another city.

References

Afterschool Alliance, "America After 3PM," web page, undated. As of July 20, 2010:
http://www.afterschoolalliance.org/AA3PM.cfm

Barrett, Scott, "Information Systems: An Exploration of Factors Influencing Effective Use," *Journal of Research on Computing in Education*, Vol. 23, No. 1, Fall 1999, pp. 4–16.

Bodilly, Susan J., and Megan K. Beckett, *Making Out-of-School-Time Matter: Evidence for an Action Agenda*, Santa Monica, Calif.: RAND Corporation, MG-242-WF, 2005. As of July 20, 2010:
http://www.rand.org/pubs/monographs/MG242/

Bodilly, Susan J., Jennifer Sloan McCombs, Nate Orr, Ethan Scherer, Louay Constant, and Daniel Gershwin, *Hours of Opportunity*, Volume 1: *Lessons from Five Cities on Building Systems to Improve After-School, Summer School, and Other Out-of-School-Time Programs*, Santa Monica, Calif.: RAND Corporation, MG-1037-WF, 2010. As of September 2010:
http://www.rand.org/pubs/monographs/MG1037/

Botcheva, Luba, Catherine Roller White, and Lynne C. Huffman, "Learning Culture and Outcomes Measurement Practices in Community Agencies," *American Journal of Evaluation*, Vol. 23, No. 4, December 2002, pp. 421–434.

Breiter, Andreas, and Daniel Light, "Data for School Improvement: Factors for Designing Effective Information Systems to Support Decision-Making in Schools," *Education Technology and Society*, Vol. 9, No. 3, July 2006, pp. 206–217.

Carrilio, Terry, "Management Information Systems: Why Are They Underutilized in the Social Services?" *Administration in Social Work*, Vol. 29, No. 2, 2005, pp. 43–61.

Choppin, Jeffrey, "Data Use in Practice: Examples from the School Level," paper presented at the Annual Conference of the American Educational Research Association, New Orleans, La., April 2002.

Cyert, Richard M., and James C. March, *A Behavioral Theory of the Firm*, Malden, Mass.: Blackwell Publishers, 1992.

deAlwis, Gina, Shaheen Majid, and Abdus Sattar Chaudhry, "Transformation in Managers' Information Seeking Behaviour: A Review of the Literature," *Journal of Information Science*, Vol. 32, No. 4, August 2006, pp. 362–377.

Feldman, Jay, and Rosann Tung, "Whole School Reform: How Schools Use the Data-Based Inquiry and Decision Making Process," paper presented at the 82nd Annual Meeting of the American Educational Research Association, Seattle, Wash., April 2001.

Fight Crime: Invest in Kids, *America's After-School Choice: The Prime Time for Juvenile Crime, or Youth Enrichment and Achievement*, New York, 2000.

Fitzgerald, Brian, and Ciaran Murphy, "Introducing Executive Information Systems into Organizations: Separating Fact from Fallacy," *Journal of Information Technology*, Vol. 9, No. 4, December 1994, pp. 288–296.

Goodhue, Dale L., "Understanding User Evaluations of Information Systems," *Management Science*, Vol. 41, No. 12, December 1995, pp. 1827–1844.

Halpern, Robert, "A Different Kind of Child Development Institution: The History of After-School Programs for Low-Income Children," *Teachers College Record*, Vol. 104, No. 2, 2002, pp. 178–211.

———, "The Challenges of System-Building in the After-School Field," in *Critical Issues in After-School Programming*, Chicago, Ill.: Herr Research Center for Children and Social Policy, Erikson Institute, University of Chicago, 2006, pp. 77–100.

Hamilton, Laura S., Brian M. Stecher, Julie A. Marsh, Jennifer Sloan McCombs, Abby Robyn, Jennifer Russell, Scott Naftel, and Heather Barney, *Standards-Based Accountability Under No Child Left Behind: Experiences of Teachers and Administrators in Three States*, Santa Monica, Calif.: RAND Corporation, MG-589-INSF, 2007. As of July 20, 2010:
http://www.rand.org/pubs/monographs/MG589/

Hasenfeld, Yeheshel, and Rino Patti, "The Utilization of Research in Administrative Practice," in Anthony Grasso and Irwin Epstein, eds., *Research Utilization in the Social Services*, New York: Haworth Press, 1992, pp. 221–239.

Hayes, Cheryl, Christianne Lind, Jean Baldwin Grossman, Nichole Stewart, Sharon Deich, Andrew Gersick, Jennifer McMaken and Margo Campbell, *Investments in Building Citywide Out-of-School-Time Systems: A Six-City Study*, Philadelphia, Pa.: Public/Private Ventures, 2009.

Herrera, Carla, and J. A. Arbreton, *Increasing Opportunities for Older Youth in After-School Programs: A Report on the Experiences of Boys and Girls Clubs in Boston and New York City*, Philadelphia, Pa.: Public/Private Ventures, 2003. As of July 20, 2010:
http://www.ppv.org/ppv/publications/assets/146_publication.pdf

Kagle, Jill Doner, "Record Keeping: Directions for the 1990s," *Social Work*, Vol. 38, No. 2, 1993, pp. 190–196.

Kerr, Kerri A., Julie A. Marsh, Gina Schuyler Ikemoto, Hilary Darilek, and Heather Barney, "Strategies to Promote Data Use for Instructional Improvement: Actions, Outcomes, and Lessons Learned from Three Urban Districts," *American Journal of Education*, Vol. 112, No. 6, August 2006, pp. 496–520.

Lauer, Patricia A., Motoko Akiba, Stephanie B. Wilkerson, Helen S. Apthorp, David Snow, and Mya L. Martin-Glenn, "Out-of-School-Time Programs: A Meta-Analysis of Effects for At-Risk Students," *Review of Educational Research*, Vol. 76, No. 2, 2006, pp. 275–313.

Marsh, Julie A., John F. Pane, and Laura S. Hamilton, *Making Sense of Data-Driven Decision Making in Education: Evidence from Recent RAND Research*, Santa Monica, Calif.: RAND Corporation, OP-170-EDU, 2006. As of July 20, 2010:
http://www.rand.org/pubs/occasional_papers/OP170/

Mason, Sarah, "Turning Data into Knowledge: Lessons from Six Milwaukee Public Schools," paper presented at American Education Research Association annual conference, New Orleans, La., April 2002.

McCombs, Jennifer S., Susan J. Bodilly, Nate Orr, Ethan Scherer, Louay Constant, and Daniel Gershwin, *Hours of Opportunity*, Volume 3: *Profiles of Five Cities Improving After-School Programs Through a Systems Approach*, Santa Monica, Calif.: RAND Corporation, TR-882-WF, 2010. As of September 2010:
http://www.rand.org/pubs/technical_reports/TR882/

Mintzberg, Henry, "Patterns in Strategy Formation," *Management Science*, Vol. 24, No. 9, May 1978, pp. 934–948.

Pittman, Karen, Alicia Wilson-Ahlstrom, and Nicole Yohalem, "Reflections on Systems Building: Lessons from the After-School Movement," *Out-of-School Time Policy Commentary*, No. 3, Washington, D.C.: Forum of Youth Development, 2003.

Proscio, Tony, and Basil J. Whiting, *After-School Grows Up: Moving Toward Universal Extended School Days in Four Large American Cities*, New York: After-School Project of the Robert Wood Johnson Foundation, 2004.

Rocheleau, Bruce, "Prescriptions for Public-Sector Information Management: A Review, Analysis, and Critique," *American Review of Public Administration*, Vol. 30, No. 4, December 2000, pp. 414–435.

Schoech, Dick, "Information Systems," in Richard Edwards, ed., *Encyclopedia of Social Work*, 19th ed., Washington, D.C.: NASW Press, 1995, pp. 1470–1479.

Supovitz, Jonathan A., and Valerie Klein, *Mapping a Course for Improved Student Learning: How Innovative Schools Systematically Use Student Performance Data to Guide Improvement*, Philadelphia, Pa.: Consortium for Policy Research in Education, University of Pennsylvania Graduate School of Education, 2003.

Tolman, Joel, Karen Pittman, Nicole Yohalem, Jean Thomases, and Ming Trammel, *Moving an Out-of-School Agenda: Lessons and Challenges Across Cities*, Washington, D.C.: Forum for Youth Investment, 2002.

U.S. Department of Education and U.S. Department of Justice, *Working for Children and Families: Safe and Smart After-School Programs*, Washington, D.C.: U.S. Government Printing Office, May 2000. As of July 20, 2010: http://www2.ed.gov/offices/OESE/archives/pubs/parents/SafeSmart

Visscher, Adrie J., and P. P. M. Bloemen, "Evaluation of the Use of Computer-Assisted Management Information Systems in Dutch Schools," *Journal of Research on Computing in Education*, Vol. 32, No. 1, Fall 1999, pp. 172–188.